Writing
for Results

*Academic and Professional
Writing Tasks*

Pearson Education ESL
Canadian Titles and Authors

Canadian Stories by Eleanor Adamowski

The Longman Picture Dictionary, Canadian ed., by Julie Ashworth & John Clark

Reading for the Write Reasons: English Reading and Writing for Advanced ESL Students by Donna Aziz-Canuel, Lynne Gaetz & Richard Pawsey

Amazing! News Interviews & Conversations by Susan Bates

Amazing Canadian Newspaper Stories by Susan Bates

Amazing 2! News Interviews & Conversations by Susan Bates

Amazing 2! Canadian Newspaper Stories by Susan Bates

Canadian Concepts, 2nd ed., Books 1-6 by Lynda Berish & Sandra Thibaudeau

English Fast Forward 1, 2nd ed., by Lynda Berish & Sandra Thibaudeau

English Fast Forward 2, 2nd ed., by Lynda Berish & Sandra Thibaudeau

English Fast Forward 3, 2nd ed., by Lynda Berish & Sandra Thibaudeau

Grammar Connections, Books 1, 2 & 3, by Lynda Berish & Sandra Thibaudeau

On Target by Keith L. Boeckner & Joan Polfuss Boeckner

On Target Too by Keith L. Boeckner & Joan Polfuss Boeckner

Target Practice by Keith L. Boeckner & Joan Polfuss Boeckner

Classics Canada: Authentic Readings for ESL Students, Books 1-4, by Patricia Brock & Brian John Busby

Coming to Canada: Authentic Reading for ESL Students by Patricia Brock & Brian John Busby

Contemporary Canada: Authentic Readings for ESL Students by Patricia Brock & Brian John Busby

Being Canadian: Language for Citizenship by Judy Cameron & Tracey M. Derwing

Focus 2: Academic Listening and Speaking Skills by Ranka Curcin, Mary Koumoulas, & Sonia Fiorucci-Nicholls

Focus 2: Academic Reading Skills by Ranka Curcin, Mary Koumoulas, & Sonia Fiorucci-Nicholls

Focus 2: Academic Writing Skills by Ranka Curcin, Mary Koumoulas, & Sonia Fiorucci-Nicholls

Writing for Success: Preparing for Business, Technology, Trades and Career Programs by Dale Fitzpatrick & Kathleen Center Vance

All Right!: A Guide to Correct English by Paul Fournier

English on Demand, 2nd ed., by Paul Fournier

English on Line, 2nd ed., by Paul Fournier

English on Purpose, 2nd ed., by Paul Fournier

This Side Up by Paul Fournier

This Way Out by Paul Fournier

Before Brass Tacks: Basic Grammar by Lynne Gaetz

Before Brass Tacks: Basic Skills in English by Lynne Gaetz

Brass Ring 1: Basic English for Career-Related Communication by Lynne Gaetz

Brass Ring 1: Basic Grammar Review by Lynne Gaetz

Brass Ring 2: English for Career-Related Communication by Lynne Gaetz

Brass Ring 2: Grammar Review by Lynne Gaetz

Brass Tacks Grammar by Lynne Gaetz

Brass Tacks: Integrated Skills in English by Lynne Gaetz

Open Book English Skills by Lynne Gaetz

Open Book Grammar by Lynne Gaetz

Open Road English Skills by Lynne Gaetz

Open Road Grammar by Lynne Gaetz

Open Window English Skills by Lynne Gaetz

Open Window Grammar by Lynne Gaetz

Bridge to Fluency by Elizabeth Gatbonton

Links: ESL Writing and Editing by Carolyn Greene & Claudia Rock

A Beginning Look at Canada by Anne-Marie Kaskens

A Canadian Conversation Book: English in Everyday Life, 2nd ed., Book 1, by Tina Kasloff Carver, Sandra Douglas Fotinos & Clarice Cooper

Reading Matters: A Selection of Canadian Writing by Jane Merivale

Word-by-Word Beginning Workbook, Canadian ed., by Steven Molinsky & Bill Bliss

Word-by-Word Intermediate Workbook, Canadian ed., by Steven Molinsky & Bill Bliss

Word-by-Word Picture Dictionary, Canadian ed., by Steven Molinsky & Bill Bliss

Take Charge: Using Everyday Canadian English by Lucia Pietrusiak Engkent

Take Part: Speaking Canadian English, 2nd ed., by Lucia Pietrusiak Engkent & Karen P. Bardy

Technically Speaking…: Writing, Reading and Listening, English at Work by Susan Quirk Drolet & Ann Farrell Séguin

Style and Substance: A Multimedia Approach to Literature and Composition by Claudia Rock & Suneeti Phadke

Read on Canada by Paul Sharples & Judith Clark

Getting it Together, Books 1 & 2, by Véra Téophil Naber

A Grammar Manual, Volumes A & B, by Véra Téophil Naber & Savitsa Sévigny

Advanced Half-Hour Helper: Puzzles and Activities for ESL Students by Joan Roberta White

Half-Hour Helper: Puzzles and Activities for ESL Students by Joan Roberta White

Making the Grade: An Interactive Course in English for Academic Purposes by David Wood

Writing
for Results

*Academic and Professional
Writing Tasks*

H. M. McGarrell
P. Brillinger

Pearson
Education ESL

DISTRIBUTED BY ÉDITIONS DU RENOUVEAU PÉDAGOGIQUE INC.

5757, RUE CYPIHOT
SAINT-LAURENT (QUÉBEC)
H4S 1R3

TÉLÉPHONE : (514) 334-2690
TÉLÉCOPIEUR : (514) 334-4720
COURRIEL : erpidlm@erpi.com

Project editor: Joyce Rappaport

Book design
and page layout:

TRIAMEDIA

Registration of copyright: 3rd quarter 2002
Bibliothèque nationale du Québec
National Library of Canada
Imprimé au Canada

ISBN 2-7613-1316-X
 234567890 II 09876543
131316 ABCD   OF2-10

WRITING FOR RESULTS
ACADEMIC AND PROFESSIONAL WRITING TASKS

INTRODUCTION 1

WRITING UNITS

Unit 1 PROCESS TO PRODUCT: A REVIEW OF THE WRITING PROCESS **5**
1. Reflecting 7
2. Prewriting 9
3. Drafting 12
4. Revising 13
5. Editing 14
6. Publishing 15

Unit 2 PARAGRAPHS AND THEIR STRUCTURE **17**
1. Paragraphs 19
2. Paragraph Patterns 21
3. Sequence of Ideas 23
4. Irrelevant Details and Digressions 25
5. Topic and Focus 26
6. Writing a Paragraph 29
7. Concluding Sentences 31
8. Transitions Between Ideas 31

Unit 3 CLASSIFICATION AND DEFINITION **35**
1. Review and Explanation of Classification 37
2. Review and Explanation of Definition 38
3. Metaphors and Similes 40
4. Getting Ready to Write 42

Unit 4 COMPARISON AND CONTRAST **45**
1. Introducing the Form 47
2. Prewriting 49
3. Topic Sentence and Outline for Comparison and Contrast Paragraphs 51
4. Clarifying and Expanding Ideas 52
5. Writing the First Draft 52
6. Peer Feedback 53
7. Revision and Editing 53
8. Final Draft 54

Unit 5 CAUSE AND EFFECT **55**
1. Review and Explanation 57
2. Some Practice Through Example Paragraphs 58
3. Getting Ideas and Drafting 61

4. Analysing and Explaining Information in a Graph 62
5. Grammar Practice in Preparation for Editing 64

Unit 6 USING SOURCES EFFECTIVELY: PARAPHRASING AND SUMMARISING **67**
1. The Paraphrase 69
2. Plagiarism 74
3. Using Quotations 74
4. The Reference Section 76
5. Summarising 77
6. Identifying the Essentials 78

REAL LIFE WRITING TASKS

Task 1 THE ESSAY **83**
1. Review 85
2. Comparison/Contrast Essay Writing 89

Task 2 ANSWERING QUESTIONS **99**
1. Short-Answer and Essay Questions 101
2. Fill-in-the-Gap, Multiple-Choice, and Sentence-Completion Questions 105
3. Learning to Deal with Time Limits 106
4. Tips on How to Answer Questions 107

Task 3 THE ANNOTATED BIBLIOGRAPHY **109**
1. Characteristics of an Annotated Bibliography 111
2. Purpose of an Annotated Bibliography 111
3. Types of Sources Used in an Annotated Bibliography 112
4. Compiling an Annotated Bibliography 113

Task 4 THE ARGUMENTATIVE ESSAY **117**
1. Purpose and Characteristics of Argumentative Essays 119
2. Developing an Argument 120
3. Examining an Argumentative Essay 122
4. Writing an Argumentative Essay 123

Task 5 WRITING A RESUME AND COVER LETTER **127**
1. Background Information: The Resume 129
2. Getting Started 130
3. The Cover Letter 138

Task 6 WRITING A BUSINESS REPORT **141**
1. General Explanations 143
2. Guidelines on the Business Report Format 143
3. A Business Case 144
4. Writing the Report 147

Task 7 THE RESEARCH PAPER **151**
1. Getting Started 153

2. Gathering Ideas 156
3. Purpose, Audience, and Topic 159
4. Developing Research Questions 160
5. Preparing to Write the First Draft 160
6. Editing and Final Copy 164

THE RESOURCE CENTRE **167**
Editing Checklist 167
Revisions from First to Final Draft 169
Peer Feedback Questions 172
Portfolio Writing 173
Library Skills 175
Cover Page 177
Selected Web Sites 178
Transitions 180
Common Errors 182
A Brief Guide to Punctuation 194
List of Irregular Verbs in English 196

GLOSSARY **199**

INDEX **206**

INTRODUCTION

Acknowledgements

We wish to express our thanks to all the ESL students and their teachers who inspired, then sampled sections in the earlier versions of this book.

We are grateful to Jean-Pierre Albert and his team for their support, and to Joyce Rappaport, our editor, for her efficient feedback and invaluable suggestions throughout the project.

We are especially thankful to Pat and Paul for always being there with their support and encouragement. To them we dedicate this book.

Introduction

To the Teachers

Writing for Results: Academic and Professional Writing Tasks presents a flexible process-oriented, task-based program of writing for English as a Subsequent Language (ESL) students or for others interested in developing academic writing skills. Its three sections provide extensive practice with rhetorical structures and academic writing conventions, sample texts that illustrate what is expected, and skill development through real life writing tasks. The first section contains six units of building blocks to help students understand and practise features of English academic style. The second section proposes seven different tasks that students are likely to encounter in their academic course work or professional situations. The third section includes varied resource and reference materials that students and teachers will likely find helpful. Numerous models on general topics are included throughout the first two sections. The general topics avoid the need for extensive background work on vocabulary and subject knowledge. They allow students to focus on the organisational and technical points introduced before applying them in their own writing.

Writing for Results: Academic and Professional Writing Tasks is based on the process approach to writing and includes pre-writing, drafting, revising, and editing activities in all the units and most of the tasks. It engages students in awareness-raising activities based on models and their previous writing experience. In turn, this encourages them to draw on their prior knowledge and relate it to each new writing experience. The text helps students develop a sense of their audience and an awareness of the need to consider purpose, audience, and topic of their writing. Finally, the text draws on recent insights into the value of collaborative learning. While some of the activities included in *Writing for Results: Academic and Professional Writing Tasks* are intended for individual work, others encourage and draw on opportunities for students to learn from each other. However, as some students may be unfamiliar with the benefits of group work, especially peer feedback, these techniques should be introduced and practised, especially at the beginning of a course. Most students readily learn to appreciate the availability of peers who help generate ideas, providing an audience for their writing or a forum for discussion of writing difficulties. They begin to see writing as communication, and peers as a resource for feedback, additional ideas, and useful suggestions.

Briefly, then, the objectives for this text are
- to prepare students to be able to write a variety of academic and real life writing tasks. For example, in needs analysis surveys in writing classes, students regularly request work with a resume/cover letter to help them prepare for the job market. Many of the tasks and skills practised in this text are transferable to business and professional situations.
- to include activities that focus on both product and process.
- to encourage students to be mindful of audience and purpose in writing.
- to develop an understanding of a variety of organisational patterns used for the development of ideas in more formal writing (e.g., definition and cause/effect).
- to practice critical reading and constructive feedback skills through peer and group interaction.
- to encourage work habits that lead students to become increasingly independent writers.
- to help students develop strategies they can use to deal with academic assignments.
- to prepare them to support their arguments and cite sources so as not to plagiarise.
- to lessen student anxiety by using models and raising their awareness of expectations.

Additional background information and suggestions for teaching and evaluation are offered in the Teacher's Manual for *Writing for Results: Academic and Professional Writing Tasks*.

To the Students

Writing for Results: Academic and Professional Writing Tasks is based on what students in our ESL classes have asked for and found helpful. One of the objectives of this text is to help you develop skills and techniques to become an increasingly independent writer. The text gives you many opportunities to practise. It also helps you understand writing conventions that help make your writing effective. This is done through activities that ask you to examine your own or your peers' writing to detect features that increase or decrease the effectiveness of the writing you produce. The activities often involve working in small groups because research indicates that university and college students can learn more from each other than from listening to lectures. A group or a partner provides you with an audience for your writing, people who share your desire to improve writing abilities and who are interested in the same topics as you are. Your peers will help you sharpen your critical thinking skills when they argue issues of opinion with you.

To achieve the greatest rewards possible from working with peers, it is important to
- respect the members in your group.
- work as a team committed to helping one another achieve the objectives of the lesson.
- participate as fully as possible.
- listen closely to one another, then ask questions to clarify meaning.
- argue about the topics–not the people–so as to maintain a harmonious atmosphere.

Remember the skills that you develop working in groups are skills that can be transferred into the workplace where much of what you do depends on your communication and people skills. In many work situations, individuals are part of a team. The success of the individuals that make up a team is closely linked to individuals' ability to interact with each other.

Features of Academic English

Writing for Results: Academic and Professional Writing Tasks gives you an opportunity to develop your ability to use academic English writing style, which might be described as
- balanced–attempts to be objective and supports ideas with evidence.
- responsible–justifies claims, understands, and credits the sources of ideas and support.
- explicit–makes clear to the reader the main ideas and how different parts of a text are related.
- formal–avoids colloquialisms, slang, and contractions.
- focussed–has a point of view or stance.

A Note on Spelling Conventions

Spelling conventions vary slightly in different countries that use the English language. Canadian spelling tends to follow British spelling conventions, but accepts some American English spellings. The resulting mixture of spelling conventions can prove confusing to native speakers and ESL students alike and result in inconsistencies. *Writing for Results: Academic and Professional Writing Tasks* reflects British spelling, but writers should be aware of the different conventions they will encounter. The traditional guideline that writers should use the spelling conventions that reflect the background of their audience is worth bearing in mind, but as internationalisation and increasing electronic communication blur geographic boundaries, writers need to be aware of these differences. Below are a few examples to illustrate the most frequently encountered differences:

British	American
acknowledgement	acknowledgment
ageing	aging
analyse, criticise, organise	analyze, criticize, organize
burnt, learnt	burned, learned
cancelled	canceled
catalogue	catalog
centre, centred	center, centered
colour, honour, labour	color, honor, labor
fulfil	fulfill
licence (n)	license (n)
organisation	organization
practise (v)	practice (v)

PROCESS TO PRODUCT:
A REVIEW OF THE WRITING

UNIT 1

Unit 1 | PROCESS TO PRODUCT: A REVIEW OF THE WRITING PROCESS

Objectives: – To identify and examine the main components of the writing process
- To practise activities at each stage of the writing process
- To reflect on and write about your own strengths and weaknesses with regard to these components

The focus of this unit is on discovering what writers do before and while they write. Start by thinking of your own ideas about and experiences with writing.

1. Reflecting

An important part of improving one's writing ability is to gain an understanding of the process.

Activity 1 Awareness Raising

Different writers approach the task of writing in different ways. If you had to write a letter or a composition, which steps would you take?

1. On your own, use point format to list briefly the sequence of steps you would follow. Then indicate which steps you find easy and which ones you find more difficult to do.
2. Working with a partner, compare your lists.
3. Discuss the similarities and differences you find and explain any points your partner does not quite understand. Revise your list if necessary.

Things to do	Easy	Difficult
get paper and pen (or: start up the computer)	X	

For many people, writing is an enjoyable and satisfying activity. For others, the idea of writing–especially writing formal letters, reports, and academic papers–produces stress. An understanding of the writing process and practice should make the activity easier.

Writing is often seen as a process consisting of a series of phases, as illustrated in the following list and discussed in the remainder of this unit.

THE WRITING PROCESS

Phase 1 - Prewriting

- gathering ideas and information
- focussing on and supporting a main idea
- organising the ideas
- planning the paper

Phase 2 - Drafting

- developing the material generated in prewriting to produce a first draft

Phase 3 - Revising

- identifying strong and weak points in your writing
- getting feedback from other writers and potential readers (peers, instructor, friends)
- rewriting the draft, probably several times

Phase 4 - Editing

- proofreading
- checking for standard use of grammar, spelling, style, formatting

Phase 5 - Publishing (optional)

In the writing classroom context, publishing can mean any of the following:

- displaying work in class
- exchanging work with another class
- arranging a poster display
- placing work on the World Wide Web
- submitting work for inclusion in a newsletter or similar type of publication

Experienced writers may not follow these phases in linear sequence but may go back and forth between phases as needed. For the purposes of discussion and practice, however, these phases are usually presented in a linear order.

> **Attention to grammar and mechanics is left to the editing phase of the writing process while earlier phases focus on gathering, organising, and presenting ideas. Premature attention to details of grammar and mechanics would likely slow down or stop the flow of ideas.**

1. Compare the five phases of the writing process, listed previously on page 8 with the list you generated in Activity 1. How similar are the two lists?
2. Discuss with your peers why you might have left out phases or included additional ones. You will have an opportunity to practise individual or sequenced phases of the writing process throughout this book. In this unit, you work through these phases to produce two descriptive paragraphs on the topic of your strengths and weaknesses in writing English.

2. Prewriting

During the prewriting phase, writers first gather ideas and information and then do preliminary planning for their composition. This phase should result in three products: a topic or thesis sentence, an outline or list of main ideas, and sufficient notes about the topic to allow you to produce a draft in the next phase.

Gathering Ideas and Information

Writers gather ideas and information in different ways. Depending on the writing task and individual preferences, some ways may be more suitable than others.

Activity 3 | Generating Ideas and Getting Information

1. In small groups, discuss when and why you would use the gathering techniques listed below.

Gathering technique	when	why
listening (lecture, radio)	radio for news on current events	very recent
watching (demonstration, television, performance, exhibit, movie)		
daily experiences (seeing, hearing, doing)		
discussion (group, interview)		
brainstorming (individual, group)		
reflection (drawing, doodling, making notes, free-writing)		
reading (for general background, specific assignments, research)		
list making (may include diagramming or grouping of ideas)		
journal writing		

2. Which of the above techniques have you used in the past? Why did you use them?
3. Select two of the techniques to gather some information and ideas on the topic of "Strengths and Weaknesses in My Writing."

Another technique for getting ideas is to ask "wh-" questions. "Wh-" questions are question words starting with *wh* or the word *how*.

| Activity 4 | Asking "Wh-" Questions |

For each of the words below, formulate one or more questions about the topic, and then try to answer them.

E.g., *Why is gathering ideas difficult for me?*

1. Why?
2. What?
3. Who?
4. How?
5. Where?
6. When?

These activities help writers list some initial ideas and relevant words that they can later use in their writing. Ideas and words need to be developed into larger chunks such as phrases and sentences. The next activity gives you some practice in doing this.

| Activity 5 | Free-Writing |

Now that you have some ideas about the topic, get ready to write for three minutes–without stopping–on the topic of "My Strengths and Weaknesses in Writing English." You will need paper, a pen, and a human or mechanical timer. Try to write complete sentences. When that is difficult, write phrases or, if necessary, individual words that come to mind when you think about the topic. Do not go back to check what you have written and do not worry about spelling and grammar. If necessary, keep writing the same word over and over again. The most important thing is that you keep writing!

How did you do? The technique you have just used, *free-writing*, is intended to help you develop fluency–the ability to write freely without pauses between words or phrases, and expressing complete ideas without stopping. The process gets easier if you use it regularly. Gradually increase the length of time you free-write to up to ten minutes.

Planning Your Writing

You should be aware of some terms and their meanings before you start to write. They are the *purpose*, *audience*, and *topic* of what you are about to write. The words are abbreviated to be called the *PAT Principle*.

Purpose

What is the purpose of your writing? What should it achieve? Should it inform, explain, enter-tain, amuse, compare, contrast, or convince? If your writing is to inform your audience, you should cover the relevant information, but if your purpose is to entertain, you will likely include anecdotes or similar material.

Audience

Who will read your writing? How much is your audience likely to know about the topic of your paper? What do you expect to be the background, age, or other features of your audience? Knowing your audience helps you to decide upon many details about your writing, including the vocabulary, sentence structure, level of formality, arguments, organisation, and approach. If you wrote about a formal subject for an academic audience, these details would be quite different than if you were writing about the same subject for a layperson. If you express an opinion to an audience that will likely agree with your point of view, you will apply a different organisation and use different arguments than you would with readers who will likely disagree.

Topic

Once you know your purpose and audience, you need to formulate a generalisation that states the main idea you wish to stress in your paper. This generalisation defines and delimits the topic and is expressed in a topic sentence. Any time you write, you need to determine what you will say to achieve your purpose with this particular audience. Next, you need to write a sentence that states your topic, whether for a single paragraph or for a paper. This general statement will serve as the working thesis for your writing. Write it down on a piece of paper and keep it visible while you work on your text and make adjustments as you proceed. (You will be getting more detailed practice with writing topic sentences in Unit 2.)

Identifying the purpose, audience, and topic gives direction to your writing and makes the planning and development of your ideas easier and less frustrating for you. As you work on your paper, keep in mind how the PAT Principle applies to your work.

Activity 6 | **Applying the PAT Principle**

Determine how the PAT Principle applies to the product of this unit, which will be a paragraph each on the strengths and weaknesses of your writing skills. What is the purpose of your writing? Who is the audience? What is your topic?

a) Purpose: _____

(E.g., do you want to tell a story, explain something, inform, or amuse?)

b) Audience: _____

(E.g., do you expect to write for peers, experts, or children?)

c) Topic: _____

(E.g., do you define your topic clearly, limiting it to a central issue, and narrowing it sufficiently to be covered well?)

Most successful writers gather the ideas and notes they collected in the prewriting phase. Then they organise them to show possible development of ideas for their writing before they move on to the drafting phase. Ideas can usually be presented in different ways and in different sequences. Some writing experts say that writers should start with their second most important point and end with their most important one. Writers may need to rearrange their ideas several times to arrive at the most effective order. Although this can be a time-consuming activity, it helps you to avoid wasting writing time later. The process of rearranging gives writers an overview of the logical progression of their ideas and allows them to decide where they might need to gather more information.

Activity 7 — Organising Your Ideas

1. Take the material you collected in the prewriting activities. Circle ideas about "strengths" and underline ideas about "weaknesses".
2. Identify the three most important points about "strengths" and the three most important points about "weaknesses".
3. List each point below and try to give an example to support it beside each point.

Strengths	Examples

Weaknesses	Examples

3. Drafting

During the drafting phase, writers get their ideas on paper in phrases and sentences, without worrying about the precise choice of words, spelling, sentence structure, or other technical details. The product of this phase is a first or *rough* draft that contains in logical order all the main ideas, based on the organisation worked out at the end of the prewriting phase. It also includes supporting ideas.

Compose a first draft describing the strengths and weaknesses you are aware of in your writing. As you write, try to frame your ideas into an organised passage but resist the urge to reread, restructure, and rewrite. For this assignment, develop one main point about the strengths and one main point about the weaknesses of your writing. (You will learn more about organising text in the next few units.) Keep writing without stopping to rearrange or polish your work, as you will be asked to do this later, during the revision phase. If the organisation plan you developed at the end of the prewriting phase does not seem to be going well, go back to prewriting and either develop more ideas or identify a different organisation plan. Try to implement this plan by using the main and supporting points you developed. You may need to go back and forth between prewriting and drafting several times until you are more satisfied with your first draft. Once you have finished your first draft, it is time to move on to the next phase in the writing process, the *revision phase*.

4. Revising

During the revision phase, writers work on improving and refining the first draft. They critically evaluate their work and may solicit feedback to help them decide where revisions might be appropriate. Learning to revise their own work is important but is often difficult for beginning writers. They may try different techniques to help them revise their work.

Activity 9 **Revision Techniques**

As a class or with a partner:

1. Look at the list of revision techniques and indicate which ones you have used.
2. Discuss which of the seven techniques is most useful for you. Explain why.

Technique	used it	new
Try to read your first draft from the perspective of your audience. Ask whether you have given enough details, whether you reflected your ideas fully, whether the sequence makes sense.		
Use the PAT Principle to review your draft: Does your draft suit its purpose? Is it appropriate for the intended audience? Is it on topic? Does it include ideas that do not belong to the topic?		
Check the topic sentence. Does it reflect your main point? Could you improve the wording?		
Look at the supporting points you make. Do they really support your topic sentence? Should you add more support?		
Consider the organisation of your ideas. Is the sequence appropriate? Is it effective?		
Ask a peer to comment (give feedback) on your draft.		
Get feedback from your instructor.		

Getting peer feedback is an activity during which you exchange your draft copy with that of one of your peers, read it, and follow a questionnaire to give your peer feedback on his or her work. Feedback may be given during peer discussion or in writing. You might want to ask your peer specific questions. For example, you might ask whether he or she can identify the topic sentence in your work. Your peer might also be able to indicate which ideas appeal to the reader and should, therefore, be developed.

Activity 10   Peer Feedback

1. Exchange your draft copy with that of one of your peers.
2. Then read your partner's draft, commenting on the following (your instructor may ask you to write down your comments or to discuss them with your partner):

   A. Who is the intended audience of your partner's draft?

   B. What is its purpose?

   C. Is there a paragraph each on *strengths* and *weaknesses* in your partner's writing?

   D. How could your partner improve the description of his or her *strengths* and *weaknesses*?

   E. Add any other comments you may have.

When you have completed your comments on your partner's draft, return it and consider the comments your partner has written for you. Think about these comments carefully and clarify any questions you may have about them with your partner. Remember that your partner is giving you his or her opinion from the perspective of the reader. The suggestions you receive are intended to help you improve your writing and to make it more appropriate for your readers. It is up to you to decide whether and how to incorporate all of these suggestions into your second draft.

Before you proceed to the next stage, you should revise your draft. Look carefully at all the observations and comments you have obtained about your draft (your own, your peer's, and your instructor's). They should help you determine which sections of your draft might need additional work. You will learn where you should add more details and where you might change the organisation of your ideas. If your draft does not include enough material or if some of your ideas are not related to the topic, you may find it necessary to return to the prewriting phase and generate additional ideas before you can complete your second draft.

5. Editing

The editing phase, also called *proofreading*, involves a detailed inspection of a text with a view to regularising its spelling, punctuation, grammar, format, and layout. The editing phase occurs when writers check for errors in grammar and mechanics. This requires careful attention to detail, both in terms of language and format. You will have an opportunity to practise several editing techniques throughout this book. The first one involves starting an Editing Checklist (see the Resource Centre), which you will use for all your assignments in this course. The items on the list will reflect weaknesses in your writing and remind you of what to look for in your writing during the editing phase. Most of the items on the Editing Checklist will relate to your own difficulties in writing, although your instructor may ask you to add some more general items that apply to you and your peers.

Activity 11 — Editing Checklist

1. Look at the Editing Checklist on page 167 in the Resource Centre. The list includes three common grammar difficulties writers experience in English. Check your final draft to make sure that it does not include problems with the three items listed. If necessary, correct your final draft.

2. Look at the Suggested Items for Editing Checklist on page 168. Check those items that cause you problems in your writing. In the spaces provided, add any additional items that you find difficult. If you know how to identify and correct the items, enter them into your Editing Checklist, and then check your draft to see if you have used these additional items correctly. As you learn more about how the other items function, add them to your Editing Checklist. Take note of comments from your teacher to identify additional items for your list. Keep adding to this list whenever you become aware of a new item, and then use it as a final checklist when you are at the editing stage of writing. The list will likely grow quite long, but as you get used to editing your work, you will find that the task becomes easier.

Activity 12 — Final Copy

If you work with a word processor on a computer, you can edit and make changes to your work quite easily. Save your file, and then run the spell checker. Make your final changes and save the file again. However, if you produced your final draft in pen or pencil, you will have to rewrite it in order to have a clean copy.

6. Publishing

At the final stage of the writing process, you share the work you produced with the intended audience. This may be done in a number of different ways and your method of presentation depends on who the audience is. One way of sharing work written for peers in a writing class is by displaying it in the classroom (see Activity 13). This is the technique that you and your peers will use for your paragraphs on strengths and weaknesses in writing.

Activity 13 — Sharing Your Work

1. Staple the two paragraphs you have written onto a sheet of coloured construction paper or another large sheet of paper. Then display it on a notice board or wall in your classroom.

2. Read all the paragraphs your peers have written and think about the *strengths* and *weaknesses* you have in common.

3. In class, discuss which common strengths and weaknesses are exhibited among the members of your class.

You have now worked through the phases of the writing process. In the following units you will have an opportunity to review and practise some of these phases and to learn additional techniques that writers use.

Summary of Unit 1

In this unit you

- were introduced to a special way of looking at writing, called process writing
- tried out some prewriting activities

- drafted your profile as a writer
- engaged in a peer feedback activity
- considered feedback from a peer to help you revise your draft
- followed some editing techniques
- shared your work by publishing it on the notice board in your class.

Alternate or Additional Topics

Describe the main characteristics of
- a good job and a bad job
- a positive attitude and a negative attitude
- an interesting movie and a boring movie
- a relaxing vacation and a stressful vacation
- an effective leader and an ineffective leader
- a developed country and an underdeveloped country

PARAGRAPHS AND THEIR STRUCTURE   UNIT 2

Unit 2 | PARAGRAPHS AND THEIR STRUCTURE

Objectives: - To review the internal organisation of paragraphs
- To examine and practise writing topic, focus, supporting, and concluding sentences
- To learn to avoid including irrelevant details
- To provide transitions to link the individual sentences

The focus of this unit is on the paragraph, its components, and its typical construction. The first activity helps you think about what you know already about the components of paragraphs.

Activity 1 | Awareness Raising

1. Read the paragraph below, entitled "Insulin (A)." Then use different coloured pens to underline each of the components mentioned in points a) to d):
   a) the introduction
   b) the conclusion
   c) the sentence that contains the controlling idea or topic sentence
   d) the supporting ideas that are part of the topic development
2. Compare your work to that of a partner. Discuss any differences in your answers and try to justify them.

INSULIN (A)

Insulin is an important hormone produced by the pancreas. This hormone is used to treat diabetes, a condition that means having too much sugar in the blood. Diabetes is a potential threat to almost every organ system in the human body: the blood vessels, the eyes, the kidneys, and the nerves. It tends to lead to a variety of illnesses, including heart attacks and strokes, kidney failure, blindness, nerve damage, or impotence. Although insulin was discovered in the 1920s, scientists are only just beginning to understand how it works.

1. Paragraphs

English academic writing is organised into paragraphs that vary in length depending on the complexity of the topic. An average paragraph has five to ten sentences and between seventy-five and one hundred and fifty words. It can appear as an independent unit or with other paragraphs as part of a longer piece of writing. Typically, it focusses on one idea and develops that idea in a linear fashion—that means the sequence of ideas progresses in a single series of steps or stages to make it easy for readers to follow the ideas presented. When a topic is too broad or complex for a single paragraph, the writer develops the discussion of the topic over several paragraphs (see Real Life Writing section, especially Task 1). Paragraphs may start with an indentation or, especially in academic and professional texts, at the left-hand margin. The visual appearance of these two formats is illustrated in A and B below.

Hiro had always thought of himself as a good student, a reasonable, responsible and reliable young man and he found it difficult to understand what was happening to him now. One day his friend asked him a question and he snapped back with an angry response. His study habits had gone "down the tubes" as his Canadian friends would say. He felt depressed and angry much of the time. Everything his host family said and did seemed unreasonable. He hated the sound of English and the way Canadians behaved. What could be wrong with him, he wondered. It is possible he was suffering from culture shock. Understanding culture shock and its causes is important ;for people living in a foreign country because if they are aware of the symptoms and how to deal with them their stay can be more fulfilling.

Culture shock is a condition that is commonly experienced by people who are living in a second culture. According to Brown (1980:81) it refers to "a phenomenon ranging from mild irritability to deep psychological panic and crisis". This implies that there can be great variations in the degree to which culture shock affects people. We could compare it to the common cold. A cold can last for two days to two weeks. Occasionally a cold can escalate into something more serious like pneumonia or bronchitis. The individual's health, habits, ability to recognize and react to the symptoms and the atmosphere surrounding the person are all factors that affect the seriousness of a cold. A multitude of factors may also be related to the degree of seriousness of culture shock. Being aware of the condition and the symptoms is an important first step in dealing with the problem.

The symptoms of culture shock are many and varied. Brown (1980) notes that some associated with culture shock are anger, sadness, loneliness, homesickness and even illness. The person may alternate between feelings of anger and self-pity according t Oberg (1993:31) identifies more detailed symptoms such as "excessive washing of ha concern over drinking water, food dishes, and bedding,...an absent minded stare, a fe helplessness" or "great concern over minor pains and eruptions of the skin". These sy all be coupled with a dreadful desire to be back home.

Both authorities agree that there appear to be stages in the successful adjustment to a and culture shock may be one of them. These include a first stage of excitement after Everything is interesting and new. People are kind and thoughtful and dote on the ne the person stays for a longer period of time, this euphoria is unlikely to last when he/ with real situations or difficulties. Obvious symptoms of culture shock may begin he time a new stage begins when the visitor becomes aggressive and even hostile to the Even when native speakers help, they do not seem to understand the difficulties. At t visitors often band together with those from their own country. They may be highly c host country and stereotype the people. If visitors do not work through this stage to

A- Block Style

Hiro had always thought of himself as a good student, a reasonable, responsible and reliable young man and he found it difficult to understand what was happening to him now. One day his friend asked him a question and he snapped back with an angry response. His study habits had gone "down the tubes" as his Canadian friends would say. He felt depressed and angry much of the time. Everything his host family said and did seemed unreasonable. He hated the sound of English and the way Canadians behaved. What could be wrong with him, he wondered. It is possible he was suffering from culture shock. Understanding culture shock and its causes is important ;for people living in a foreign country because if they are aware of the symptoms and how to deal with them their stay can be more fulfilling.

Culture shock is a condition that is commonly experienced by people who are living in a second culture. According to Brown (1980:81) it refers to "a phenomenon ranging from mild irritability to deep psychological panic and crisis". This implies that there can be great variations in the degree to which culture shock affects people. We could compare it to the common cold. A cold can last for two days to two weeks. Occasionally a cold can escalate into something more serious like pneumonia or bronchitis. The individual's health, habits, ability to recognize and react to the symptoms and the atmosphere surrounding the person are all factors that affect the seriousness of a cold. A multitude of factors may also be related to the degree of seriousness of culture shock. Being aware of the condition and the symptoms is an important first step in dealing with the problem.

The symptoms of culture shock are many and varied. Brown (1980) notes that some of the feelings associated with culture shock are anger, sadness, loneliness, homesickness and even physical illness. The person may alternate between feelings of anger and self-pity according to Brown. Oberg (1993:31) identifies more detailed symptoms such as "excessive washing of hands, excessive concern over drinking water, food dishes, and bedding,...an absent minded stare, a feeling of helplessness" or "great concern over minor pains and eruptions of the skin". These symptoms may all be coupled with a dreadful desire to be back home.

Both authorities agree that there appear to be stages in the successful adjustment to a new culture, and culture shock may be one of them. These include a first stage of excitement after arrival. Everything is interesting and new. People are kind and thoughtful and dote on the new visitor. If the person stays for a longer period of time, this euphoria is unlikely to last when he/she has to deal with real situations or difficulties. Obvious symptoms of culture shock may begin here. At this time a new stage begins when the visitor becomes aggressive and even hostile to the host country. Even when native speakers help, they do not seem to understand the difficulties. At this stage the visitors often band together with those from their own country. They may be highly critical of the host country and stereotype the people. If visitors do not work through this stage to new understandings, they may leave and go home. Next, the visitors may take a stoic attitude that says "This is my problem and I have to bear it." They may develop a sense of

B- Indent Style

The basic internal organisation of paragraphs includes three main components:
- a topic sentence
- four to eight supporting sentences
- a concluding sentence.

Writing that consists of a single paragraph contains all of these components in that one paragraph; longer texts expand the components over several paragraphs. Although you will write at the paragraph level in this unit, you can see in the following table how the construction of a paragraph compares to the construction of a multi-paragraph text.

Paragraph	Essay
Introductory, attention-getting sentence that expresses the topic	**Introductory paragraph:** General statements Thesis statement
Supporting sentences	**Body paragraphs:** Topic sentence Supporting sentences Concluding sentence/transition to following paragraph Topic sentence Supporting sentences Concluding sentence/transition to following paragraph Topic sentence Supporting sentences Concluding sentence/transition to following paragraph
Concluding sentence	**Concluding paragraph:** Restatement sentences Closing sentence

Multi-paragraph writing will be discussed in more detail later on. For now, look more closely at paragraph organisation and topic sentences.

2. Paragraph Patterns

The organisation of paragraphs in English academic or professional writing typically consists of distinct patterns to help readers follow the ideas presented. For example, in a *general to specific* paragraph organisation, the writer gives specific facts and illustrations to support general statements. The first sentence of the paragraph, the topic sentence, indicates the general subject and the specific parts of that general subject that will be developed. The sentences that follow then support, explain, or develop these parts. Finally, the last sentence serves to conclude, summarise, emphasise, or reinforce the topic sentence. The complete paragraph forms a unit that might be represented like this (the examples that follow assume between five and six supporting sentences):

Paragraph Pattern 1 - Development by Supporting Details

Sentence 1	Topic sentence
Sentence 2	More specific information about the topic
Sentence 3	More specific information about sentence 2
Sentence 4	More specific information about sentence 3
Sentence 5	More specific information about sentence 4
Sentence 6	More specific information about sentence 5
Last sentence	Concluding statement about the topic

A different treatment, called *development by points*, might address two or three points, each one offering support for the controlling idea expressed in the topic sentence, as illustrated in Paragraph Pattern 2 below:

Paragraph Pattern 2 - Development by Points

Sentence 1	Topic sentence
Sentences 2 and 3	Point number one: Specific supporting details
Sentences 3 and 4	Point number two: Specific supporting details
Sentences 5 and 6	Point number three: Specific supporting details
Sentence 7	Concluding statement about the topic

A third paragraph pattern develops the controlling idea through an *example*:

Paragraph Pattern 3 - Development by Example

Sentence 1	Topic sentence
Sentences 2 to 6	Example, illustrating and expanding on the topic sentence
Sentence 7	Concluding statement about the topic

Activity 2   Comparing Paragraph Patterns

1. Look at the three paragraphs on Insulin (A, above and B, C, below).
2. Note in the margin or on a separate piece of paper which pattern (development by supporting details, development by points, or development by example) each reflects and how closely each paragraph follows this pattern.
3. During class discussion, listen to your peers' analysis of the paragraph and be prepared to justify your own.

INSULIN (B)

Insulin is an important hormone produced by the pancreas. The hormone regulates the blood sugar level in the blood. It enables cells to use blood sugar by passing blood sugar into the cells if energy is required, or into storage in the liver if no energy is required. If there is too little of the hormone insulin in the body, a condition called diabetes can occur. Diabetics have too much sugar in the blood, which is a potential threat to almost every organ system in the human body: the blood vessels, the eyes, the kidneys, and the nerves. It tends to lead to a variety of illnesses, including heart attacks and strokes, kidney failure, blindness, nerve damage, or impotence. Insufficient insulin in the body can be treated. In milder cases, diets low in sugar and back-up in the form of pills may help stimulate the pancreas to produce more insulin. More serious cases may require injections of insulin from animals or manufactured insulin. Although insulin was discovered in the 1920s, scientists are only just beginning to understand how it works.

INSULIN (C)

Inconsistent production of the hormone insulin can negatively affect a person's sense of well-being. For several weeks, Fran had been plagued by a feeling of fatigue. At first she thought it was just a reflection of her hectic schedule. After all, most of her friends also seemed to complain of feeling tired. Then, as her skin seemed increasingly itchy and her eyes became sore by the time she finished work in the evening, she told herself that it was the result of spending too much time indoors. When she mentioned her symptoms during a routine check up at the doctor's office, her doctor immediately prescribed a series of tests for her. A few days later, she was called back to the doctor's office to learn that her symptoms were due to a condition called diabetes. This condition can develop when the pancreas produces too little of the hormone insulin in the body. Although more serious cases may require injections of insulin from animals, Fran's doctor felt that a diet low in sugar, supplemented by medication, would likely stabilise her body's production of insulin to help her regain her sense of well-being.

In academic texts, paragraph development can be organised by supporting details, through points, examples, or a combination of these.

| Activity 3 | **Looking Closely at Paragraph Development** |

In small groups, discuss how the three types of paragraph development differ. Then respond to the following questions:

1. Which type of paragraph development do you prefer to use in your academic writing?

   Why?_____

2. When do you think you would most likely use paragraph development by example?

   _____

3. Sequence of Ideas

Sequencing ideas in a paragraph is often a difficult task for developing writers. Even experienced writers spend considerable time crafting their paragraphs at the revision stage. Look for paragraph patterns in your reading, especially academic reading, to help you understand how writers organise and support their ideas.

Activity 4 — Sequencing Ideas in a Paragraph

1. Look at the paragraph on "The Topography of Japan" below. Determine whether it follows Paragraph Pattern 1, 2, or 3.
2. Explain your choice to your peers.

The Topography of Japan
Michiyo Fujita

Two aspects of Japan's topography have a significant effect on its population density. First, Japan consists of four main islands and over 3,900 smaller islands. Many of these smaller islands are uninhabitable. A second aspect of topography that has contributed to the high population density is that 72 percent of Japan is covered by mountains. This leaves only 377,728 square kilometres of its surface for its over 120 million people to live. The result is that Japan has been left with a population density of 316 people for every square kilometre, one of the most densely populated countries in the world.

Activity 5 — Identifying the Sequence of Ideas in a Paragraph

Read the sentences below. Then number them to indicate the sequence in which they should be ordered if they are to follow Paragraph Pattern 1.

___ It consists of four main islands: Hokkaido, Honsyu, Shikoku, and Kyusu and over 3,900 smaller islands, some of which are not inhabitable.

___ Japan has a varied topography that helps make it one of the most densely populated countries in the world.

___ Japan ranks 42nd in the world in terms of its geographic size, but 7th in terms of its population.

___ This results in a population density of 316 people for every square kilometre.

___ Mountains cover about 72 percent of the land, leaving little of its surface area of 377,728 square kilometres for its population of just over 120 million people.

Activity 6 — Develop Your Own Paragraph

Option 1: Write a paragraph similar to the one in Activity 4, describing a different country.

Option 2: Use the notes below to write a paragraph that follows Paragraph Pattern 1 or 2. Develop additional ideas if necessary.

Strict Teachers Help Students Develop Their Potential

- an important influence
- a role model
- help a student prepare for future responsibilities
- the teacher's high expectations encourage strong performance

1._____

2._____

3._____

4._____

5._____

4. Irrelevant Details and Digressions

English academic writing prefers paragraphs in which each sentence follows directly from the previous sentence, without digressions, i.e., without moving away from the topic and focus identified in the topic sentence. Sentences that digress from the topic can obscure the main idea the writer wants to convey, distract readers, or make the paragraph more difficult to follow.

| Activity 7 | Recognising Sentences that Digress |

Read the paragraph "The Topography of China" below. Look for and underline sentences that do not fit into the main topic. In a discussion with the whole class, explain why these sentences are irrelevant in the context of this particular paragraph.

The Topography of China
Ping Lee

China's surface slopes down like a staircase from west to east in four steps. The top of the staircase is the Qinghai-Tibet Plateau. This is a very beautiful place. Its snow-capped peaks and glaciers reach elevations of more than 4,000 metres. The Inner Mongolian, Loess, and Yunnan-Guizhou plateaus and the Tarim, Junggar, and Sichuan basins represent the second step of the staircase. In this area, elevations reach between 1,000 and 2,000 metres. There is great variation in climate in this region. Further down the staircase, at an altitude of about 500 to 1,000 metres, are the Greater Hinggan, Taihang, Wushan, and Zuefeng mountain ranges. Together with the North China Plain and the Middle-Lower Yangtze Plain they represent the third step of the staircase. This area has a high population density and there is a great deal of agriculture. East of this area is an extension of land into the ocean, the continental shelf, which forms the fourth step of the staircase. With most of China's rivers flowing from west to east, many waters have brought great quantities of mud and sand to this lowest point of the topographical staircase of China.

> Sentences that digress may be difficult to identify, especially in your own writing. Although they are rarely completely irrelevant to the topic, they do not develop the topic but distract from it.

Practice makes perfect.

An important key to clear paragraph organisation in effective academic and professional writing is a topic sentence that lets readers know the writer's focus and attitude toward the topic right away. The formulation of a topic sentence requires writers to think carefully about what they wish to say and to determine their attitude toward the topic. The following section helps you develop your understanding of topic sentences.

5. Topic and Focus

The topic is what the writer is talking about, and is often indicated in the title. A topic sentence indicates an idea or attitude that the writer plans to adopt. While a topic may be general and open to a number of different perspectives, a topic sentence shows clearly what the perspective taken is and how the topic has been narrowed. Writers show what their particular "angle" or focus on the topic is. Determining the angle and focus may take considerable time and may include prewriting activities. Once they have found their focus, writers can articulate a topic sentence, which will help them determine what kind of support they need to include in the paragraph and how they will narrow a potentially broad topic. In summary, the topic sentence can be defined as a sentence that introduces the topic and focusses, narrows, or limits it.

An examination of the characteristics of topic sentences suggests that it is easier to talk about what they are *not*. For example, topic sentences are not formulated as a question but will often be the answer to a question.

A question such as

    X   What are the advantages of air traffic deregulation?

might lead to the possible topic sentence:

    √   <u>Air traffic deregulation</u> brings many advantages to the traveller.
               Topic   Focus

To support this topic sentence, the writer will need to list several advantages that individuals who travel by plane can expect as a result of air traffic deregulation.

The following sentence does not represent a topic sentence:

In this paper, I am going to discuss the Jaguar, a very special car.

Although this sentence opens up a general topic and represents a statement of intention or purpose (which is useful to include), it cannot replace the topic sentence. By contrast, look at this next sentence:

The Jaguar is one of the best-designed cars in the world.

This statement deals with the same topic but is phrased to express a specific attitude toward the Jaguar. The statement represents an acceptable topic sentence. To support it, the writer will need to describe the Jaguar's design and demonstrate the advantages that come from such a design. Compare this with another potential topic sentence, one that would require facts for support:

My city is one of the cleanest cities in North America.

To support the controlling idea expressed, the writer might provide comparative information about measures of cleanliness in different North American cities.

> Note that clear topic sentences help writers understand what kind of support they need to offer. Once they have provided this support, their writing task is completed.

Activity 8 — Practice with Topic Sentences and Their Focus

With a partner, discuss
1. the following pairs of sentences to determine which of each pair of sentences is suitable as a topic sentence;
2. what the writer's focus is;
3. how the writer might develop each topic.
   - 1a) Most beer bottles have twist tops.
   - 1b) Twist tops make beer bottles difficult to open.
   - 2a) The benefits of the World Wide Web.
   - 2b) The World Wide Web is a useful tool for information retrieval.
   - 3a) Education and poverty are important concepts.
   - 3b) The key to eventual elimination of poverty in North America is education.
   - 4a) Many communities operate recycling programs.
   - 4b) Recycling programs result in financial and social benefits for communities.
   - 5a) In this paper I will discuss how to get the most out of historical photographs.
   - 5b) A careful look at the people in a picture, their clothing and accessories, and the background shown reveals historical details relevant to the photograph.
   - 6a) Many influences may contribute to shaping children as they develop into adults.
   - 6b) Parents exert a major influence on a young child.

| Activity 9 | **Recognising Potential Topic Sentences** |

Work with a partner.
1. Examine the following sentences to decide whether they would be acceptable as topic sentences. Give reasons for your choices.
2. Suggest how the sentences that are unsuitable as topic sentences might be changed to become topic sentences.
   A. The disadvantages of keyless entry cars.
   B. Can pills energise people?
   C. Why more organ donors are needed.
   D. Computers have revolutionised the banking industry.
   E. The effect of pop culture on the world economy.
   F. In this paper I will discuss the history of the local Chamber of Commerce.
   G. Healthcare issues in rural areas of your country.
   H. Pop culture has affected the world economy in at least three ways.

In the following activity, practise your understanding of how topic, focus, and paragraph pattern interact.

| Activity 10 | **Topic Sentences with a Focus** |

1. Working on your own, choose four of the subjects below, and write a topic sentence with a focus for each of them.
2. Working in groups of three, discuss each other's topic sentences and examine whether they include a narrowed topic and a focus.

Banking in the 21st Century	Culture as a Commodity
Leisure Time	Citizens' Rights and Responsibilities
The Power of Marketing	The Politics of Resources
The Automotive Industry	Access to Education

3. Select the three or four best topic sentences written by members of your group, and write them on the board for class presentation.

| Activity 11 | **Niagara Falls - Pattern of Paragraph Development** |

1. Read the following short paragraph on Niagara Falls.
2. Identify its topic sentence, focus, and paragraph development according to the paragraph patterns outlined in this unit.

Topic sentence:_____

Focus:_____

Paragraph pattern:_____

Niagara Falls
François Bélanger

Niagara Falls attracts a wide variety of visitors all year round. Each winter, tourists enjoy looking at the iced-up falls and the colourful Festival of Lights. In the spring, they come to admire the cascades of water from melted ice that tumble over the falls and the blossoms in the nearby peach and cherry orchards. During the summer months, tourists delight in watching the falls, maybe from one of the tour boats, and the falling water which produces sprays of mist that drench unsuspecting tourists and create rainbows above them. In the fall, visitors like to combine their visit to the falls with a tour of the fall foliage. The change of the seasons may alter the way the falls look, but the views are always stunning.

Outlining is often part of the prewriting process. An outline is a framework or plan for a paragraph or a longer text. It lists the main and supporting points of a text and shows their sequence. Outlining helps writers organise their ideas in point format and limit major changes in organisation later on.

Activity 12   Outlining a Paragraph

Outline the paragraph on Niagara Falls.

Topic sentence: _____

Support 1: _____

Support 2: _____

Support 3: _____

Support 4: _____

Concluding sentence: _____

6. Writing a Paragraph

Writing a successful paragraph takes preparation and a number of identifiable steps. Follow each of the steps defined in Activity 13.

Activity 13   Preparing to Write

1. Select one of the topics you worked on in Activity 10.
2. Discuss each of the following steps in groups of three.
3. Then, on your own, complete each step for your own topic. You may want to try two or three different topics before you choose the most promising one.

Step 1: Identify the audience. Who will read your paragraph?

Audience: _____

Step 2: Understand the purpose. What effect do you want your text to have on readers? (E.g., is your goal to inform, to stir up emotions, or to convince?)

Purpose: _____

Step 3: Narrow your topic. Review how you narrowed the topic. Make sure that you have found the most suitable focus, and then state your focus:

_____

Step 4: Create a topic sentence. Revise the topic sentence that you created in Activity 10 to suit the readers and purpose identified in Steps 1 and 2. Plan on writing one paragraph (unless your teacher assigns a longer assignment).
Revised Topic Sentence: _____

_____

As a next step in writing your paragraph, work out an outline in point format. Use the pattern illustrated in Activity 14 below to indicate your main points and your supporting points.

| Activity 14 | **Outlining** |

Organise your main points and ideas or examples to support them into a paragraph outline (fill in as many points as you need for your paragraph).

Main point 1: _____

Support 1: _____

Support 2: _____

Main point 2: _____

Support 1: _____

Support 2: _____

Main point 3: _____

Support 1: _____

Support 2: _____

Now you should be ready to start writing your paragraph, using the points you listed in your outline. Your instructor will let you know whether you should write your draft paragraph on the computer or on a separate sheet of paper.

7. Concluding Sentences

The concluding sentence is the last sentence your audience reads. It is your opportunity to leave your readers with a strong impression of the topic and its focus. This may be achieved in at least two ways:

a) Writers repeat the main idea of the paragraph through different wording.

b) Writers formulate a conclusion based on the information they provided in the paragraph.

| Activity 15 | Analysis of Concluding Sentence |

1. Look back at the paragraphs entitled "Insulin (A)" and "Niagara."
2. Determine which method was used to conclude each paragraph.
3. Write a different concluding sentence for each.

Insulin (A)_____

_____

Niagara _____

_____

Read one of your concluding sentences aloud to the class and listen to the sentences your peers have written. When you hear a sentence that you like, complete items 4 and 5:

4. Indicate why you like the concluding sentence. _____

_____

5. Suggest the characteristics that make an effective concluding sentence. _____

_____

This might be a good opportunity for you to go back to the paragraph you wrote above at the end of Activity 14 and to have another look at your concluding sentence. Is it effective according to your own analysis in item 5? If necessary, change the sentence to make it more effective.

8. Transitions Between Ideas

Carefully developed ideas, expressed through expertly crafted sentences, are unlikely to convince readers unless those ideas are logically connected. Connecting words between sentences tend to allow readers to follow the writer's thinking by showing the relationship between one idea and the next. If there is little or no connection between ideas, readers are likely to find it difficult to follow the development of ideas and may well turn their attention to something else.

Writers can choose from four basic groups of mechanical devices to connect ideas:
- Repeating key words and phrases
- Employing transition words or expressions
- Using pronouns or demonstratives
- Constructing parallel forms

The writers' choices depend on the effect they wish to achieve. Selecting the most appropriate option from these basic groups may be difficult initially, but writers develop their skills through practice.

The paragraph on Insulin (A) at the beginning of this chapter contains a number of useful transitions. The paragraph is reproduced below for your convenience. The words and phrases in **bold** are used to establish connections between sentences.

INSULIN (A)

Insulin is an important *hormone* produced by the pancreas. *This hormone* is used to treat *diabetes*, a condition that means having too much sugar in the blood. *Diabetes* is a potential threat to almost every organ system in the human body: the blood vessels, the eyes, the kidneys, and the nerves. *It* tends to lead to a variety of illnesses, including heart attacks and strokes, kidney failure, blindness, nerve damage, or impotence. Although *insulin* was discovered over a half century ago, scientists are only just beginning to understand how *it* works.

Activity 16   Analyse the Connections

1. Read the paragraph on Insulin (A).
2. Pay special attention to the words in **bold** and how the writer uses them to connect ideas from one sentence to the next.
3. Use arrows to show which words are linked. In the second sentence, for example, the demonstrative pronoun *this* refers back to "hormone," which is the focus of the first sentence.
4. Discuss with your peers
   a) what type of connector is used in each pair of linked words;
   b) what type of connectors you have used in your own writing.

The paragraph on Insulin (A) makes repeated use of pronouns to connect ideas. These pronouns need to be used carefully to avoid ambiguous or misleading connections. Look at the following potentially misleading connections:

The students wanted to write their exams before their final papers were due. This required a lot of preparation time. (What does *this* refer to?)

Similarly, pronouns should not be used to avoid naming an agent:

They said that the exam would be on a Saturday evening. (Who are *they*?)

Using Pronouns as Connectors

Use the pronouns indicated to connect the sentences below.

it   those   its   they   these

a) Scientists hypothesise that the first people to settle North America came from Western Asia about 12,000
years ago. ~~Scientists~~ *They* hypothesise that the first people crossed over using a small land bridge from northern

Asia, then travelled down to America. The first people were the only group for thousands of years.

b) Over a million people visit Paris every year. The cultural attractions and atmosphere of Paris are

like a magnet to people from all over the world.

c) Some political leaders argue that bilingual education should not be available in the United States.

Political leaders who make this argument claim that bilingual education is inefficient and expensive.

Later units in this book will show other techniques that help create clear transitions between ideas expressed in a text. A summary of useful transitional words is in the Resource Centre section on page 180.

Activity 18 **Revising Your Draft**

1. Reread the draft version of your paragraph. Pay special attention to the following:
   a) Sequence of ideas
   Are your ideas arranged logically? Can readers easily follow the development? Did you give readers sufficient detail to enable them to follow your ideas? If necessary, rearrange the progression or the details in your draft.
   b) Connectors
   Are the different ideas in your paragraph linked clearly? What connectors did you use?
2. Discuss your changes with a peer and ask him or her whether your revisions make your paragraph easier to read.
3. Consider any suggestions your peer might offer to help you improve your paragraph.

Activity 19 **Editing Your Paragraph**

1. Look for digressions in your paragraph.
2. Check the grammar in your paragraph. Use your Editing Checklist to look for mistakes you often make.
3. If you work on a computer, use the spell checker.
4. Make the necessary corrections. Then follow your teacher's instructions about handing in your paragraph (i.e., print out or submit on diskette).

Summary of Unit 2

In this unit you
- reviewed the organisation of paragraphs
- focussed on the internal organisation of paragraphs
- examined different types of paragraph structure used frequently in academic and business writing
- learned to look for sentences that are not directly relevant to the main topic
- practised writing strong topic sentences and concluding sentences
- started to pay careful attention to how sentences are connected within a paragraph.

CLASSIFICATION AND DEFINITION

UNIT 3

Objectives: - To discover the uses of classification
- To explore three types of definition
- To learn about metaphors and similes
- To practise using them to develop paragraphs

The focus of this unit is on definition as a writing pattern. Classification and different types of definitions are illustrated and explained, based on how they are used in writing.

1. Review and Explanation of Classification

Classification is a way of organising information and expressing or explaining ideas. You can think of it as a way of dividing things into groups to help your reader understand your point more easily. For example, just as large stores are divided into departments, and countries are divided into provinces or states, you can divide or classify experiences or concepts to show their scope or range. Dogs can be classified into breeds, and novels can be classified as mystery, romance, science fiction, or adventure. Classification is a useful method of focussing a paragraph or even developing an essay. It is important when dividing or classifying a concept to keep the divisions complete and distinct.

Diagramming classification and division is a helpful way to brainstorm on some topics. As you can see in the example about dogs, there can be a number of levels to these divisions:

Dogs		
Working Breeds	Sporting Breeds	Herding Breeds
Great Dane	Bloodhound	Australian Cattle Dog
Newfoundland	Dachshound	Belgian Shepherd
Saint Bernard	Foxhound	Old English Sheepdog
Siberian Husky	Greyhound	Shetland

Activity 1 | **Awareness Raising**

1. Read the following paragraph, which uses classification as the method of development.
2. Underline the topic and circle the focus in the topic sentence.
3. List the four kinds of physically based security devices.

Security and Technology
Mohamed Jamil

Security for electronic devices has become an important issue in the information age, and four physical characteristics could be used to restrict access. Each of these characteristics is unique to the individual who desires entry. Used with computer technology, the characteristics can be entered as identifying data to give people access to information or sites that for various reasons might require restricted access. Fingerprint identification is the first. Not a new technology, it has been used for years to identify criminals. Having a computer that is capable of checking the fingerprint of the person would mean that only a person whose fingerprint was registered on the computer could get into a site. Second, a voice print would allow for only the person with that unique voice signature to enter. The retinal or iris pattern of the eye is also completely different from one individual to the next and could be used in the same way. Finally, DNA research has reached the point at which it may be possible to use a DNA print to screen out all but the person or persons with permitted access. Using these uniquely individual patterns to identify people at bank machines, on the Internet, or at places of work with security concerns would make it impossible for people of ill will to use criminal means to gain access.

Activity 2 · Practise Brainstorming Divisions

1. Using the topics listed below, work in pairs to list as many logical divisions as you can. See if your group can develop more than one level to the divisions.
2. Then move into groups of four to compare notes, adding ideas and layers of divisions that you have gained from the others.

Topics

Communication Devices	Types of Businesses	Excuses for Late Assignments
University Majors	Doctors	Reasons for Studying English

Activity 3 · Writing a Paragraph Describing Divisions

1. Choose one of the topics above and write a paragraph explaining the classifications or divisions. Give examples.
2. Share your paragraph with a partner. Then ask your partner if the writing and divisions are clear.
3. Edit your paragraph on your own. Rewrite it and hand it in.

2. Review and Explanation of Definition

Definitions are explanations of a term and are used to state the meaning of that term. Definitions are common for short-answer questions on an exam. Definitions are also often expected as parts of answers to essay-type questions on exams and in essays. Defining your terms can be an important component of many academic writing tasks. How you define your terms depends on the task, the audience, and the purpose. There are different types of definitions that may be required.

1. Read the details given for the three different types of definitions given below.
2. Identify and discuss the differences in meaning with a partner.
3. Which types of definitions have you not used before? Why?

Short Definition

A short definition usually uses a *synonym* (a word that has the same meaning) or a *classification* (a short explanation of a word). You should choose a synonym that is easier to understand than the word that you are defining. It should also take the same grammatical form as the word you are defining. In a short definition, you may also include information about classification or a brief explanation and an example. The more abstract a term is, the more information you may need to give your readers to get across the meaning.

Example of a Short Definition:

A house is a building used as a living space to shelter a family or a group of people in a relationship of some kind.

Extended Definition

An extended definition uses supporting material to illustrate a concept and helps readers understand the concept. It may include
a) the synonym, classification, or short explanation found in a short definition
b) examples, both positive (i.e., showing what the concept is) and negative (i.e., showing what it is not), and
c) an analogy (i.e., an explanation of something that compares it with something that is in part similar).

The passage below shows different ways of supporting an extended definition. All of these would likely help the reader to understand the term the writer wants to define and would lessen the likelihood of confusion.

Example of an Extended Definition:
A house is a building or living space, which is often used to shelter a family, people in a relationship, or individuals living together for a special purpose (e.g., to study, to save money). A house has one or more rooms that may be designated for particular purposes, for example, a kitchen, a living room, a bedroom. Some houses are detached, some are semi-detached, and some are joined in rows and called row houses or townhouses. A hotel is not a house. It shelters people and often families. However, it is used for temporary shelter, for numbers of unrelated people, and for commercial gain by the owner. An office tower is not a house, as it is used only to shelter business operations and those involved in them. People are there for working purposes only. A house, however, is where people eat, sleep, raise children, and spend most of their free time. Houses come in many styles and are built of many materials. This is because availability of materials and adaptability of structures to geographical requirements lead to many differences. Today houses are like cocoons. People see them as a place to keep out the world's distractions so they can have a haven in which to grow and change or perhaps hide from a hostile environment.

Stipulative Definition

A third type of definition is called a stipulative definition. This type of definition limits the scope of the concept being defined to meet the needs of a specific situation (e.g., research, law). Stipulative definitions are found in expert sources and quoted in academic and other texts. Writers use them in research papers, studies, reports, or legal documents to specify the meaning of a term in order to limit the way in which the writer treats the topic. A stipulative definition allows writers to establish common ground with their readers, which in turn helps them discuss the topic according to certain criteria.

> **Example of a Stipulative Definition:**
> External validity refers to whether or not the results of research can be generalised from the samples used in the research to the general population. Even though a certain treatment used in the research appeared to have a particular effect with the sample used it may not be able to be generalised to wider populations because typical circumstances may be quite different from those in the study. This would mean that the study would not be externally valid.

Activity 5   Thinking About Definitions

Discuss the following questions with a partner. Then compare your answers with those of the whole class.

1. What are some similarities among the three types of definitions discussed? What are some differences?
2. In what types of writing would you use each of the above types of definitions?
3. Who would be your audience?
4. What would be your purpose?
5. Answer the following about the extended definition:
   a) What is the purpose of a negative example?
   b) "Today houses are like cocoons" is an analogy. What is its purpose in this definition?

3. Metaphors and Similes

Explanation

Metaphors and similes are analogies that are written sometimes for poetic effect and sometimes to help a person understand an idea that may be difficult to express. They can be helpful in extended definitions, particularly in definitions of abstract terms. A metaphor gives a name or descriptive term to another object or action when the term is imaginatively but not literally applicable. Some examples:

Metaphor: Love is a GIFT.

How is love a gift?

It sometimes comes as a surprise.

We can give it or receive it.

Love may look one way on the outside and quite different as we open it up and live with it.

Metaphor: She was a GUIDING LIGHT to her family.

How was she a guiding light?

She guided her children along the path of life.
Her behaviour showed people her care for them.
People found that her words and example helped them to see things in a new way.

A simile is also figurative language, but with similes the writer makes the comparison explicit by using *like* or *as*. Look at the following examples.

Simile: The horse ran through the streets LIKE A TANK on a war field laying waste to everything in its path.

How is a horse like a tank?

It is strong and heavy.

It can move over rough ground.

It may knock people down if they get in the way.

Simile: My father is LIKE AN OAK TREE.

How can a father be like an oak tree?

An oak tree is tall and strong, and so is my father.

An oak tree protects people from rain and storms. My father protects me from the storms of life.

An oak tree provides homes for birds and squirrels. My father provides me with a home.

When writers develop a metaphor or a simile, they find it useful to spend some time thinking of ways in which the analogy is true. If they list the ways, they will have more ideas to work with later on.

Activity 6   **Working with Metaphors and Similes**

1. Choose one of the terms below or use a term that you have discussed with your instructor.
2. Circle the term you want to work with.
3. List five ideas for metaphors or similes.
   patriotism   friendship   war   family   computer   language   patience

   Idea 1: _____

   Idea 2: _____

   Idea 3: _____

   Idea 4: _____

   Idea 5: _____

4. On a separate sheet of paper, list ways in which the term you have chosen is like these things.

Your page might look like the following example:

A) Metaphors for "Father": lighthouse, tree, (university,) king, grocery store

B) Ways in which a father is like a university:

A father is like a university because we can learn things when we are with him. We learn not just one thing but many different things like finance, science, and language. We only learn what we are willing to learn. Sometimes we may be tested on what we have learned. Many other people learn from my father–others in my family, people who work with him. There is a cost in learning from my father. Sometimes it costs me patience. It may cost me time away from my computer, the TV, or my friends. It costs me some pride sometimes to admit that he may know something that I do not know.

4. Getting Ready to Write

Activity 7   Developing Ideas

1. As a class, brainstorm some words for which you will write a definition.
2. Record them in a place where everybody can see them (e.g., the chalk board).
3. Choose one of the words to develop into an extended definition below.

Your word: _____

Gather ideas by listing and brainstorming.

4. List as many synonyms for the word as you can find. You may need to use a dictionary or thesaurus for this task.

_____ _____ _____

_____ _____ _____

5. Can you classify the word in any way? _____

_____

6. List as many positive examples as you can for the word. Try to find examples that say what the word *is* (i.e., that are positive) rather than what it is not (i.e., negative).

_____

_____

_____

_____

7. List one or two negative examples._____

_____

8. Brainstorm metaphors and similes for your term. _____

_____

_____

Activity 8   Writing an Extended Definition

Using your ideas on a separate piece of paper, write a one-paragraph, extended definition for the term you have selected.

Activity 9   Reviewing and Revising

In small groups of two or three,
1. Discuss and explain the ideas you have gathered in your extended definition paragraph of Activity 8.
2. Look at the examples and analogies, asking your partners how they think your examples and analogies help them understand the term.
3. Ask your peers for other suggestions.
4. Keep notes of their feedback, and then revise your work.

The comparison of ideas gives you feedback on how readers might understand your text. Anything readers in your group misunderstand or comment on should make you rethink how you have presented your ideas and how you could formulate them more effectively.

Activity 10   Editing

1. Check the grammar in your paragraph of a definition, paying particular attention to mistakes you often make (use your Editing Checklist). You may catch more mistakes if you read the paragraph backwards, one sentence at a time.
2. Check the format. Is it double spaced? Neat? Easy to read?
3. If you work on a computer, use the spell checker.
4. Hand in your revised draft for feedback and/or marking from your instructor.

Summary of Unit 3

In this unit you
- learned the importance of definitions in academic work
- learned about different types of definitions and some of their uses
- practised writing a paragraph explaining a classification or division
- wrote both short and extended definitions of words or terms.

Alternate or Additional Activities

1. Each person in the class should write a word on a piece of paper. It might be a new word learned recently that is difficult to understand. Or perhaps it might be a word that came up in a reading used in class. Until you have worked with easier terms, do not choose a technical term or scientific term that would be extremely difficult to explain. Put the pieces of paper in a container or bag. Each person should pull out one of the words. If you choose your own term, return it to the bag and choose again. Write an extended definition for your word. In groups, teach your word to the others by reading your definitions. Choose the one definition that you found most challenging. Read that definition to the whole class.

2. Alternately, you might write three short definitions for an unusual word that you have found in the dictionary. One definition should be the correct one, while two others should be false definitions. In groups, read your three definitions and ask the others to determine which one is the correct one.

COMPARISON AND CONTRAST

UNIT 4

Unit 4 COMPARISON AND CONTRAST

Objectives: - To review the rhetorical pattern used to compare and contrast
- To explore the use of a Venn diagram for brainstorming
- To write a paragraph comparing or contrasting two topics
- To give peer feedback, then edit the paragraph
- To practise the use of transition markers for comparison and contrast

The focus of this unit is on comparison and contrast writing. The first activity will let you review previously practised rhetorical patterns before you start to explore comparison and contrast in greater detail.

1. Introducing the Form

| Activity 1 | Awareness Raising–The Paragraph |

Respond to the following questions. Then compare your answers with those of your peers.
1. What is a paragraph?
2. Where in the paragraph would you usually expect to find out what its topic is?
3. How do most well-organised paragraphs end?
4. What is the purpose of the middle section of a paragraph?

The paragraph patterns practised in Units 1 and 2 are the widely used forms of narrative and description. Comparing and contrasting information requires a different paragraph pattern: that of comparison and contrast. Two basic patterns are commonly used. The first one is called block style. With this pattern, there are two sections: one that shows similarities and one that shows differences; or one for each thing to be compared, as the illustrations below indicate. A second pattern is called the point-by-point (or alternating) pattern. In this pattern, the writer selects the categories of comparison and discusses the two topics using each category.

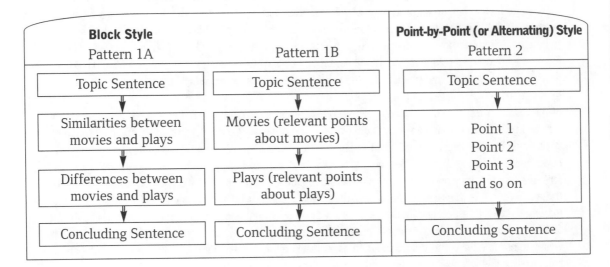

Block Style		Point-by-Point (or Alternating) Style
Pattern 1A	Pattern 1B	Pattern 2
Topic Sentence	Topic Sentence	Topic Sentence
Similarities between movies and plays	Movies (relevant points about movies)	Point 1 Point 2 Point 3 and so on
Differences between movies and plays	Plays (relevant points about plays)	
Concluding Sentence	Concluding Sentence	Concluding Sentence

Read the following examples. You will be asked to answer some questions about them in Activity 3.

Example 1:

Different but Good
Alexandra Perez

Although two of my favourite teachers, Ms. Eliot and Mr. Lewis, were very different in many ways, they had an important impact on my life because of the qualities they shared. Ms. Eliot was tiny and dark. Her movements were quick and dramatic. She wore bright, flamboyant clothes that attracted attention to her every movement. Her extroverted nature was exhibited in the personal stories she told and her obvious feelings for the subject matter and us. Mr. Lewis, on the other hand, was tall and heavy. His movements were slow and lethargic. He wore dull, common clothes, grey and blue, unlike her trendy colourful and sometimes wild combinations. In contrast to Ms. Eliot's personality, Mr. Lewis was introverted and quiet. It was difficult to know how he felt about things. Everything was matter of fact and organised in his classes, with no elements of drama and emotion. In spite of these differences, they were both excellent teachers who cared passionately about their students and their material. They were conscientious, organised, and always well-prepared. I loved them both, enjoying their differences and appreciating their commitment to teaching and to us.

Example 2:

Ms. Eliot and Mr. Lewis: A Study in Contrast
Tameera Makkeree

Although two of my favourite teachers, Ms. Eliot and Mr. Lewis, were different in many ways, both had an important impact on my life because of the qualities they shared. They certainly had their differences in appearance, style, and personality. Ms. Eliot, who taught English, was petite, dark, and small-boned. She looked like a house sparrow in search of food as she flitted around the room, dark eyes tracking the responses of the students and her easy smile lighting up her face. Her clothes were as flamboyant as her nature. She always wore brightly coloured swishing skirts, and a multitude of beads and jewellery meant that each movement was accompanied by a flash of colour and sound. On the other hand, Mr. Lewis, my history teacher, was tall, fair, and heavyset. His eyes were blue and as indecipherable as the sea. He never appeared to be attending to us; however, many a student was surprised to learn that he did not miss a thing. His fair hair was a nondescript colour, neither blond nor brown. Unlike Ms. Lewis, his clothes were dull and ordinary, grey slacks, white shirts, and predictable blue ties. His movements were predictable too. Perhaps because of his six-foot-two frame and big bones, moving was heavy work. Whatever the reason, he rarely left the front of the room, pacing in a small rectangle between his desk and the door. The differences in appearance were echoed in the differences in personality and teaching style. She was extroverted, a ham actor, and told amazing stories and jokes that kept us all enthralled and brought the characters to life for us with dramatic readings. Mr. Lewis, however, rarely changed the tenor of his voice, and was quiet and introverted when illustrating the history of a country, the world, or a famous person in organised charts, graphs, and feedback loops. In spite of these differences, each was passionate about the subject taught, each was kind and caring about the students treating them with respect and fairness, and each was conscientious about preparing for classes. These shared qualities provided each classroom with an atmosphere where learning abounded, and where students felt willing to risk and were encouraged to attain goals. Teachers who care about their students and work hard to enhance learning will always be successful whatever their appearance or personality differences.

Using the example paragraphs, discuss and review the qualities of a good paragraph. Mention some of the points to be considered in comparison and contrast.

1. Underline the topic sentence of each paragraph in the reading.

   Does it introduce the topic? Y / N

   Does it show opinion or intention? O / I

   Is it a complete, grammatical sentence? Y / N

   Does it have a focus? Y / N

2. Are all the supporting details relevant? Y / N

3. What means does the author use to make the details interesting and believable?

4. Does the paragraph have a concluding sentence? Y / N

5. What pattern is used in each paragraph–block or alternating?

6. Underline the transition markers or other words that are used to show similarities or differences.

7. Are there any sentences used specifically to move the reader from one idea to another, or are all the sentences simply supporting the topic sentence?

8. How does the author achieve the purpose and reach the audience?

Activity 4   Qualities of a Good Paragraph (Review)

Briefly review Unit 2 to refresh your memory about the qualities of a good paragraph. When you write your next paragraph, keep the points you have learned in mind and apply them when you write.

2. Prewriting

Prepare to write a comparison-and-contrast paragraph by choosing a topic.

Activity 5   Choose a Topic for Comparison and Contrast

If you find it difficult to think of a topic, you might consider one of these suggestions:

two movies	the food from two countries
two sports	city and country life
two friends	owning and renting a house

Write down your topic: _____

The following activities will suggest techniques to help you narrow your topic.

Activity 6   **Brainstorming a List of Categories**

Use the grid below to list ideas about your topic.

Category of comparison	Topic A:	Topic B:
1.		
2.		
3.		
4.		

Activity 7   **Exploration Through Venn Diagram**

A Venn diagram is a diagram that uses closed curves, especially circles, to represent sets. Use the Venn diagram below to explore differences and similarities between the two ideas or items to be compared. Use side A for one item, side B for the other. Characteristics that are shared by both items are shown where the two curves overlap.

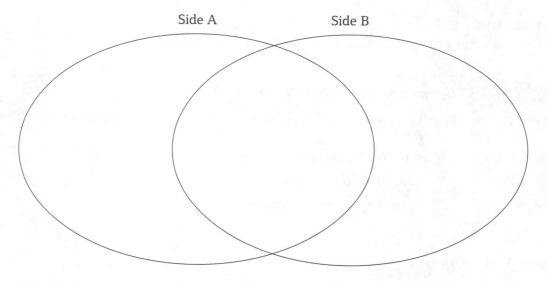

Side A   Side B

If necessary, your instructor will review the qualities of a good topic sentence, supporting details, and concluding sentences. Pay careful attention, and ask questions if you are not sure that you understand the points made. Take notes for future reference.

3. Topic Sentence and Outline for Comparison and Contrast Paragraphs

Make sure you
- identify the two items or ideas that are being compared
- indicate whether you will be looking at similarities and/or differences
- take a stand.

Not

There are many differences between life in urban and rural areas.

but

Living in an urban area offers more variety than living in the country because of the many educational, cultural, and athletic opportunities available.

Write your topic sentence here:

_____

_____

Activity 8   **Check Your Topic Sentence**

Look carefully at the topic sentence you wrote above. Look for the following and place a check mark (√) in front of each statement that you think applies to your topic sentence:

A topic sentence should
___ state the topic
___ indicate a clear focus
___ contain opinion or intention
___ not be a question
___ be *one* complete, grammatically correct sentence
___ be interesting and lead the reader to want to go on

Activity 9   **Identifying Supporting Ideas**

List the points and examples you will use to support your topic sentence and put them in the order in which you will use them.

Supporting Point 1_____

Example/ illustration_____

Supporting Point 2_____

Example / illustration _____

Supporting Point 3_____

Example / illustration _____

4. Clarifying and Expanding Ideas

The use of specific transition words helps writers clarify the relationships between the ideas they express. Try to remember what transition words you know to help you express likenesses or differences between two ideas. Your instructor may ask you to review some of these transitions as a class activity. To learn more about this topic, you may consult the list in the Resource Centre, pages 180-181.

Activity 10	Practice with Transition Words

In small groups, discuss the topics you have chosen for the comparison-contrast paragraph. Use the following examples of transitions and connectors to express similarities and differences orally. As you discuss each topic, try to engage in a real discussion, agreeing and disagreeing with each other, and adding points that others may not have thought about.

Examples of sentences using transitions that express similarities:
1. *similar to*   Similar to Niagara Falls, Victoria Falls attracts many tourists.
2. *both....and*   Both Southern Ontario and South Africa produce fine wines.
3. *like*   Like the Niagara Peninsula, the Cape Town Peninsula has many wineries.
4. *likewise*   Niagara's ice wine is becoming famous. Likewise, its white wines are becoming well-known.

Examples of transitions that may be used to express differences:
5. *unlike*   Unlike the Niagara region, the Cape Town area does not produce ice wine.
6. *whereas*   Whereas the Cape Town Peninsula is close to where the Atlantic and Indian Oceans meet, the Niagara Peninsula is between Lake Ontario and Lake Erie.
7. *in contrast to*   In contrast to Cape Town, the Niagara area is not close to the ocean.
8. *but*   The Niagara Peninsula is in Canada, but the Cape Town Peninsula is in South Africa.

Activity 11	Ideas for Your Paragraph

Use the following questions to consider the ideas you will use in your paragraph.
1. Can your ideas be grouped into categories for point-by-point organisation?
2. Are they interesting?
3. Do you have illustrations or examples to support each point?
4. Are any of them off topic?

5. Writing the First Draft

The objective of the first draft is to get the main points down on paper and to have an initial idea of how these points flow. Changes to the points and the sequence in which they are expressed can be made more easily once they are written down.

Activity 12   Writing Your First Draft

1. Write your first draft on a separate piece of paper or use the computer.
2. Put the date and your name in the upper, right-hand corner.
3. Remember to double space your writing so that you will have room to make changes.
4. Use some of the transition words that you used in your oral discussion. Your paragraph should contain about 150 words.

6. Peer Feedback

A first draft needs to be evaluated critically so that you can decide how it may be improved. Many writers find it difficult to evaluate their own work. Peer feedback is one way to get suggestions on how to revise a first draft to improve its effectiveness in terms of its intended purpose and audience.

Activity 13   Feedback on Paragraphs

1. Share your paragraphs in small groups by reading them aloud to each other.
2. Discuss each in terms of the following questions. The writer should ask the others each question and make notes on paper about changes or suggestions to improve the paragraph.
   A. What did you like best about the paragraph? Why? Who do you think is the intended audience? What do you think the writer's purpose was?
   B. Does the topic sentence identify the topic? Does it express an opinion or intention? Is it one complete sentence?
   C. Are all the supporting details relevant? Is the paragraph rich in details or does the author need to develop any of the ideas in more detail?
   D. Is there a concluding sentence? Is it interesting?

7. Revision and Editing

The suggestions writers receive from peers help them get a sense of how readers might understand the ideas expressed in the paragraph. This insight should help them decide how to revise their work. However, whether or not writers act on the changes suggested by their peers is up to them.

Activity 14   Revising Your Paragraph

1. Reread your paragraph and work to make it more effective and better organised. If you write on the computer, save the revised version in a new file. If you work with pen and paper, make all your changes with a different coloured pen so that the teacher can see how you have tried to improve your writing.
2. Check your paper for grammar errors and spelling mistakes. If you are working with a word processor, do a spell check.
3. Check to see if you have used a variety of sentence structures.
4. Make sure that you have included some of the transitions discussed in this unit.
5. Read the paragraph again and think about your word choices. Try to avoid words like *big*, *little*, and *nice*; find more effective synonyms.
6. Read the paragraph aloud and listen to the sound of your writing. Does it sound smooth? If you hear sudden stops and starts, you may have used too many short sentences. Also, you may hear an error that you did not see when reading your writing.

Things to Remember When Revising Your Paragraph:

1. A paragraph should focus on one topic and contain supporting ideas and illustrations or examples to make the idea clear and interesting for the reader.

2. The first sentence, commonly called a topic sentence, should state the topic, focus, and opinion that will follow in the paragraph.

3. The last sentence should restate or summarise the ideas presented and leave the reader interested in the content.

4. Comparing two topics means looking at similarities, noting the characteristics they share, and contrasting their differences. It is useful to think about categories of the topic or aspects of the topic that form a basis for comparing two things. These categories can be used to give a logical sequence to your ideas, whether you decide to use block or alternating style to organise your paragraph (see page 47, activity 1).

8. Final Draft

The feedback from your instructor can provide another opportunity for you to revise your paragraph before you write the final version. Read your instructor's comments carefully and ask for clarification if you do not understand them all.

Activity 15	Your Final Draft

Rewrite the paragraph in clear and legible writing or, if you are working on a computer, make your final changes, do a spell check, and check the formatting before you hand in a final copy.

Summary of Unit 4

In this unit you
- reviewed the organisation of a paragraph
- examined some examples of comparison and contrast in paragraph writing
- practised using comparison and contrast as a pattern of organisation to write a paragraph.

Alternate or Additional Activities

1. Interview a person from a culture different from your own. Discuss an aspect of culture that is interesting for you. Some examples are body language, festivals and celebrations, systems of government, parenting, or dating and marriage. You may find it useful to think about the topic and list some questions you want to ask. Some people make notes when gathering information through interviews; others use a tape recorder and listen, making their notes afterwards. Next, list at least three or four possible categories of comparison. Make an outline for a paragraph of contrast using the alternating pattern. Write one paragraph about your topic using the alternating pattern. On your own, find a partner to read what you have written, and discuss any ways in which it could be improved.

2. Meet with a friend and discuss your goals for the next few years. How are they different? How are they similar? Write one paragraph. Use block style and discuss the ways in which your goals are similar and different. Meet with a small group and read your paragraphs aloud. Take a few minutes when you have finished to discuss similarities and differences in the group.

CAUSE AND EFFECT

UNIT 5

Unit 5 | CAUSE AND EFFECT

Objectives: - To identify cause and effect
- To practise the discussion of problems, their causes, their solutions
- To present possible solutions
- To describe information presented in a graph

The focus of this unit is on writing cause-and-effect texts. A broad range of situations can be viewed in light of their underlying causes and effects, which may be real or hypothesised.

1. Review and Explanation

Each day we use our ability to analyse why something has happened or what may result if we take a certain course.

Activity 1 | Awareness Raising

1. Look at the statements below. Determine the cause and effect of an action or state.
2. Add three examples of your own.
3. Present your examples to the class.

    A. An aging population contributes to increasing health costs.

    B. Many traffic accidents occur as a result of poor driving habits.

    C. Run-off from agricultural pesticides poisons the drinking water.

    D. _____

    E. _____

    F. _____

When individuals have decisions to make in life, they often think about the effects of various options before making a final decision. They analyse the situation, discuss the possible effects (both beneficial and negative), and make recommendations based on the analysis. Cause-and-effect analysis is likely one of the most common ways of approaching a topic. It is a method that people use even as children, when they first ask the question "Why"!

Teasing tiger causes tears.

Business writing, academic writing, and examinations require writers to explain and discuss the causes of the problem, its effects, and some possible solutions. A case analysis in business, a research paper on the French Revolution, or a lab report studying the impact of acid rain on plant life would all use this type of organisational pattern. In some instances, causes and effects can be independent of each other. If this is the case, writers do not need to be concerned about the order of the material. It can be arranged to suit the audience, or causes can be put in order of importance. At times, however, there may be causal relationships that must be described in chronological order because there is a chain of events in which the one cause and its effect leads to another cause and effect. For example, acid emissions from smokestacks lead to acid rain, which in turn causes some lakes to become more acid. This leads to the inability of plants and fish to survive and causes the death of the lakes, which in turn leads to the inability of fishermen and tourist operators to carry on business, finally affecting the economy of the region. This example shows a causal chain and is similar to a process.

The Domino Effect

To develop a paragraph or an essay using this organisation pattern requires writers to think carefully about both immediate and more remote causes and effects. Sometimes a chain of events may occur in which an effect may become a cause leading to another effect. If the assignment is a one-paragraph assignment, writers may need to decide whether to focus on the causes or the effects. In an essay, it may be possible to consider one of these or both facets.

2. Some Practice Through Example Paragraphs

Some of these points may seem rather complex and abstract. Three example paragraphs will illustrate the main points and help make the ideas more concrete.

Activity 2	Awareness Raising

Read Example Paragraph A below. As you read it, bear in mind the explanations about cause-and-effect writing. You will be asked to answer some questions about the paragraph after you have read it.

Example Paragraph A

Victory
Zahra Mohamed

Many important decisions led to my graduating "cum laude." My first decision was to organise my time to avoid falling behind in my studies. Each assignment was blocked out in my timetable, the final due date identified and the project broken down into components, which would be finished by a certain date. This decision allowed me to hand in my university papers on time and with sufficient research that the ideas were interesting and well-thought-out. A second decision was to be sure that there was some time in my schedule each week for fun with my friends and enough flexibility to do something that was important for me. Being somewhat flexible and able to have fun meant that I did not grow resentful of my studies. Going out with my friends and being able to do things on the spur of the moment alleviated stress and gave a freshness to my work. Finally, the decision to set priorities for my life each year had a significant effect on my success. Each year after the final marks came in, I sat down and thought about my priorities for the coming year. One year, for example, I decided that my marks in statistics needed to go up and I set that as one of my priorities. Having made statistics a priority, my goal was to raise my mark from 78 to 82 over the next year and I did. Understanding my weaknesses and strengths and deciding what my priorities were stood me in good stead when I reached university. Combining an ability to set priorities, the discipline of managing my time well, and allowing myself time for enjoyment all helped me to graduate from university with high honours, a lot of friends, and a happy disposition.

Activity 3   Questions

Work with a partner to answer the following questions.
1. What were the three causes or reasons that ensured the author's success in university?

a) _____

b) _____

c) _____

2. What aspects of the paragraph are characteristics of a well-organised paragraph?

_____

_____

3. What words in the topic sentence indicate that the paragraph will discuss causes?

_____

4. Underline any words in the paragraph that connect ideas and make the paragraph coherent.
5. Double underline any words the author uses to signal causes or reasons.
6. What technique(s) does the author use to conclude the paragraph?

_____

_____

Read Example Paragraphs B and C. Again, bear in mind the characteristics of cause-and-effect writing and be prepared to answer some questions after you have read the paragraph.

Example Paragraph B

Changing Family Groups
Nadia Dewjee

For many reasons, the model of the extended family that was common in early Canada has diminished to the point of extinction. In the past, many families relied on parents and children to assist in farming enterprises. For this reason, one child usually stayed on in the family home to help with farm chores or perhaps built a home on part of the parents' land. In the case of city folk, they may have had to help in the family store or business and lived with their parents. There were no government-subsidised daycare centres, so in both situations the parents and grandparents shared not only in building up the economic welfare of the family or clan but also in child-rearing. Most people now live in cities and work for large companies. To get ahead it may be necessary to relocate to get a better job. Or they may be transferred to new jobs far from the family home. Finally, today's society values independence. Older people want to be independent of their children and children in North America are generally raised to and are expected to live on their own by the time they reach their late twenties. Although it may at times be difficult, these cultural expectations act as strong motivation for children and parents to live on their own rather than in homes with extended family. Type of employment, government programs such as daycare, and cultural expectations are just three of the many reasons why most North Americans live in nuclear rather than extended families.

Example Paragraph C

Getting Ahead
Luo Lui

Most young people aspire to a university education because of their expectations of its effects on their future. First, some think a university degree on a resume affects the kind of consideration they will be given when applying for a job. If a potential employer has a choice between a person with a university education and one without, they believe that the employer will choose the person with the degree. A second effect considered important to students is the social network of friends, professors and employers who can influence our job search and make it more successful. Students also see a third effect as important. That is the variety of skills picked up as a result of studying in any field that are transferable from situation to situation. For example, in university students learn to read and select out the important material, to analyse and synthesise information, to write essays and reports, to critique ideas and research, and to develop time-management skills. These are just a few of the skills learned in university that can be applied in any field of work. Understanding that these possible results of a university education widen their possibilities for future success leads many young people to compete for a place in a university program.

Activity 5 — Thinking About Cause-and-Effect Paragraphs

Your instructor will let you know whether you should discuss the following questions with the whole class or with a partner.
1. Decide which paragraph discusses causes and which one discusses effects.
2. Underline any words that signal the use of that organisational pattern.
3. Identify the logical order that the ideas follow. Some of the possible choices for logical order in cause and effect are *chain order* (which follows a chain of causes and effects); *chronological order*; *order of importance*. Go back to the beginning of this Unit for a discussion of possible logical orders if necessary.

3. Getting Ideas and Drafting

Activity 6 — Developing Ideas

Choose either topic A or B below, and follow the instructions. You will first work on your own for a few minutes, and then team up with a partner to discuss your work.

Topic A: A Special Event	Topic B: Success
Think of one event in your life that had a great impact on your future. Fill in the grid below with some of the causes/reasons for that event and the effects that it had on your life/ character/future behaviour. Meet with a partner and discuss the causes that led to the event and the effects that it had on your future.	Think of a time when you had a great success. Fill in the grid below as you think about the causes/reasons for your success and the effects that success had on your life/character/future behaviour. Tell your partner the causes of your success and some of the effects that the success had on your life or character.

Life Event or Success: _____

Causes	Effects
Cause 1	Effect 1
Cause 2	Effect 2
Cause 3	Effect 3
Cause 4	Effect 4

| Activity 7 | Drafting a Cause-and-Effect Paragraph |

1. Study the information you collected in Activity 5 and determine whether chain order, chronological order, or order of importance is most appropriate for your material.
2. Write a first draft of a cause-and-effect paragraph to practise the relevant technique.

4. Analysing and Explaining Information in a Graph

In academic work, one is often expected to read material in graphs and tables and explain or interpret it. The following section will give you some practice doing that. You will examine the graph, think about and discuss the information contained in it, and then write a paragraph explaining the information and discussing possible causes for its patterns.

Canadians frequently talk about the weather. Often they complain about winter, wishing they could go somewhere else. The statistics in the bar graph below show some regional vacation patterns in Canada.

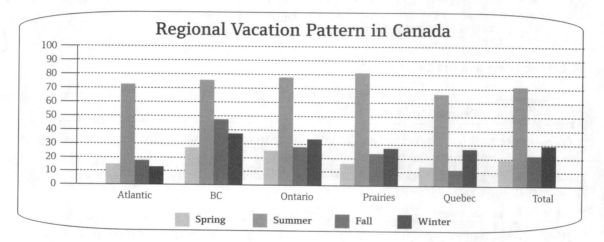

| Activity 8 | The Weather and Its Effect on Vacation Trends |

1. Look at the bar graph that indicates the regional vacation patterns in Canada. If you have access to the Internet, you may wish to go to http://www.pnr-rpn.ec.gc.ca/air/index.en.html for Climate Information for Canada.
2. In small groups, discuss the patterns that you see in Canada as a whole and the variations among the different provinces listed.
3. Keep notes on the ideas that are discussed in your group. Some of the questions you should consider include the following:
   a) What do you think are some of the causes for these patterns?
   b) How does the weather affect vacation trends?
   c) What effect does winter weather have on Canadians' vacation plans?
   d) What causes Canadians to take their vacations when they do?
   e) How might regional industries and occupations affect vacation patterns?
   f) What might cause people in some regions to take more vacations than people in other regions?
4. Think of additional questions that may help you to understand the situation.

Activity 9   Developing a Plan

Working on your own, develop a plan based on the following steps:
1. Decide whether you will explain the graph in terms of causes or effects.
2. List at least three supporting ideas for your paragraph, and then consider what type of logical order you will use.
3. Number the ideas in the order you will present them in your paragraph.

Supporting Point 1: _____

Supporting Point 2: _____

Supporting Point 3: _____

4. Select the logical order most suitable for the development of your ideas:
   a) chain order
   b) chronological order
   c) order of importance

You may need to go back to pages 57-61 for a discussion of different orders of development in a cause-and-effect paragraph.

After you have completed these prewriting activities, you should have several ideas about how to develop a paragraph on regional vacation patterns in Canada.

Activity 10   Writing a First Draft on Vacation Patterns

Write your rough draft for the paragraph. Remember to begin with a topic sentence that introduces the topic, includes your opinion or intention, and has a clear focus. You should also have at least three supporting ideas and examples, illustrations, or explanations for each. Finally, write a concluding sentence that summarises the ideas and leaves the reader interested.

Activity 11   Reviewing Ideas and Organisation

Read your paragraphs to one another in groups of three (one person reading, two listening and giving feedback).
1. Listen carefully to how clearly the ideas are expressed.
   - Did the writer accurately discuss the information in the graph?
   - Is the order of ideas logical?
   - Has the writer used chain, importance, or chronological order?
   - What did you like most about the paragraph?
   - What suggestions do you have for improvement?
2. Consider the organisation of the paragraph itself.
   - Does it have an effective topic sentence?
   - Are the supporting ideas accurate? Clear?
   - Does the writer explain the points well and use examples or illustrations?

The discussion of your own and some of your peers' paragraphs should help you decide how to revise your paragraph. Be sure to ask for clarification if you do not understand their suggestions before you revise your paragraph.

Revising

1. Read your paragraph, and then consider any suggestions made by your partners.
2. Determine how you can best use their suggestions on content and organisation to improve your paragraph.
3. Make the revisions on your first draft.

5. Grammar Practice in Preparation for Editing

Once writers have a well-organised draft that includes the ideas they want, they need to edit their work for grammatical accuracy, spelling, and format. A short exercise will help you focus on some editing issues.

Activity 13 **Fill in the Blanks with One of the Following Words or Phrases**

causes	*is caused by*	*because*
results in	*results from*	*so*
leads to	*is the result of*	*because of*
is one cause of	*one effect of*	*as a result*

a) Air pollution _____ _____ _____ car emissions.

b) Air pollution _____ _____ _____ _____ car emissions.

c) The rain was very heavy. _____ _____ _____ the accident occurred.

d) Smoking _____ lung cancer.

e) High cholesterol frequently _____ _____ heart disease.

f) One _____ _____ stress is lowered immune response.

g) Air pollution _____ _____ car exhaust.

h) She eats a well-balanced diet, _____ she is very healthy.

i) _____ she eats a well-balanced diet, she is very healthy.

j) She stayed home _____ _____ the snowstorm.

> **Remember that if you say A causes B, you are making a very strong statement. It sounds as if there is no question about it and as though this cause may be the only cause. When writing about causes and effects, it is wise to word things more carefully if there might be other possible explanations. Here are some ways to do that.**

Car emissions **may cause** lung cancer.

Car emissions **can cause** lung cancer.

Car emissions **are one possible cause** of lung cancer.

One of several possible causes of lung cancer is air pollution.

It appears that air pollution causes lung cancer.

Studies indicate that air pollution **may cause** lung cancer.

These results suggest that lung cancer may be caused by air pollution.

Activity 14   Final Editing

1. Check your work for errors in grammar, punctuation, and format. Above all, check your use of words that indicate cause and effect.
2. Use the Editing Checklist in the Resource Centre if you have been working with it.
3. Check for statements that are too strong and change the wording to show that your interpretation is only one of several possibilities.
4. Try reading your work one sentence at a time, starting at the end. This process sometimes will help you to see errors in your writing more easily. It is worth a try.

Summary of Unit 5

In this unit you
- practised using cause and effect as a pattern of organisation for a paragraph
- interpreted a graph that contains information related to causes and effects
- wrote an explanatory paragraph describing the information in the graph
- worked on important academic writing points that are particularly important in answering exam questions and writing essays.

Alternate or Additional Assignments and Topics

1. Working with graphs
   a) Go to the library or look on the Internet for a graph or table describing information from your home country. Look for information that points out causes or effects of some event or phenomenon that is of interest to you. Print out or photocopy the graph or table. Remember to identify the source of the material and the author, if any. If it is from the Internet write down the Web site address. Read the information included in the graph carefully and analyse what you see. Make notes in the side margins if needed.
   b) Write a short paragraph describing the information in the graph.
   c) Read your draft with a partner and work to improve it.
   d) In groups of four, meet to share your graphs and paragraphs. In your group, discuss which graph had the most interesting information. Which was the most unusual? Which was most important as a world concern? Why?
   e) Have your group report to the class the information that was the most interesting. Tell why.

2. Choose one of these alternative topics and write two paragraphs, one discussing the causes and another discussing the effects of your topic. For some of these topics, you will need to narrow your focus.

working mothers	jealousy	overcrowding in cities
preserving the environment	friendship	AIDS
nationalism	war	immigration
compulsory army service	stress	cheating on exams
losing my temper	being patient	air (or: road) rage

USING SOURCES EFFECTIVELY: PARAPHRASING AND SUMMARISING

Unit 6 | USING SOURCES EFFECTIVELY: PARAPHRASING AND SUMMARISING

Objectives: - To practise paraphrasing and quoting material from sources when using them to support your own ideas in an essay
- To identify the elements of and method for writing a summary
- To become aware of how to avoid plagiarism
- To learn to cite your reference sources

This unit shows how to paraphrase and quote the writing of experts or writers, incorporate the work or ideas of others into your own writing, and credit the original source. It also discusses plagiarism and provides guidelines on how to avoid plagiarising through quoting the source or using one's own words. The unit shows how to summarise long texts into smaller texts that retain only the essential information of the original, longer text. It concludes with some practice exercises on writing a reference section.

1. The Paraphrase

A paraphrase is a kind of summary that restates an original text in the words of the person who writes the paraphrase. A paraphrase might refer to a sentence, part of a sentence, a paragraph, or several paragraphs. What is important to remember is that the paraphrase has to reflect the exact meaning of the original passage. A paraphrase will likely be as long as or longer than the source it replaces.

| Activity 1 | Awareness Raising |

Look at the two sentences below. With a partner, discuss how the two differ.

A. Individuals may register a proprietorship or partnership with the Ministry of Consumer and Business Relations by completing a simple computer card available from the department and paying $11.00.

B. For $11.00, individuals can register their business with the Ministry of Consumer and Business Relations.

Paraphrases serve a number of purposes:
- to provide a shortened version of the core ideas of a text;
- to change the language or style of the original;
- to demonstrate that the writer has read and understood the original;
- to make the original more comprehensible;
- to clarify complex or technical passages.

Paraphrases usually have specific characteristics. They
- represent the original ideas accurately and completely, without reflecting the writer's personal bias; but
- are expressed in the writer's own words;
- show that the writer has read and understood the original passage;

- include a reference to their source;
- may reduce the length of the original passage;
- reflect effective sentence structure and appropriate grammar, mechanics, and usage;
- acknowledge the source.

Activity 2   More Awareness Raising

Read the passage entitled "Writing as a Process" below. Pay particular attention to material the writer has incorporated from other sources. Be prepared to answer some questions after reading the passage.

Writing as a Process
Peter Schmidt

Using the process approach, you should not just write on a given topic in a restricted time period and hand the composition in for the teacher to correct. Instead, you should develop a text through a series of steps, interacting with peers and the teacher as readers and consultants. The process involves some type of prewriting activity such as brainstorming, discussion, debating, reading, or outlining. Students write their first draft, and then, in small groups with their peers, read one another's texts and ask for feedback on the content and organisation of ideas. A second draft is then produced, incorporating any new insights and revisions. The final stage in the process is editing for mechanical or grammatical errors, formatting, and other conventions. After this stage, a final draft is handed in for grading. The crucial supports that instructors give their students using this approach are "time to try out ideas and feedback on the content of what they write in their final drafts" (Raimes, 1983, p. 10). Some of these teacher-researchers (Horowitz, 1986; Nunan, 1991) contend that a focus on product achieves better results than a focus on process.

References

Horowitz, D. (1986). What professors actually require: Academic tasks for the ESL classroom. *TESOL Quarterly* 20 (3), 445-462.
Nunan, D. (1991). *Language Teaching Methodology*. New York: Prentice Hall.
Raimes, A. (1983). What unskilled ESL students do as they write: A classroom study of composing. *TESOL Quarterly* 19 (2), 229-258.

This example follows the APA conventions of referencing sources. Other formats include: MLA, Chicago, Turabian Style. The Resource Centre, page 178 suggests some Web pages that show the format of these styles.

1. After reading the passage on process writing, work with a partner to identify the ideas that have been taken from other writers. Underline the quotation, circle the paraphrase.
2. What information is included to allow the reader to identify the source of material that is not the author's?

In the text? _____

In the references? _____

3. What techniques are used to set out this information (e.g., typing conventions, punctuation)?

_____

Examples

As we have pointed out, paraphrasing is a technique that involves stating or expressing the ideas of others in the writer's own words. Examples A and B below help illustrate the differences between an original text and its paraphrase.

Example A - Original Text	Example A - Paraphrase
"Lying is one of the crucial issues in family life. Imagine how complicated and awkward it would be if we could never trust that people meant what they said. It would be impossible if we had to check and verify everything that we were told." Ekman, P. (1989). *Why Kids Lie*. New York: Penguin Books, p. 5.	According to Ekman (1989:5), one of the most important issues of family life is lying because it would be difficult and embarrassing if we were unable to believe what people told us. We would not likely be able to make sure that everything people said was true. **or** Because it is difficult and embarrassing when we cannot believe what people tell us and because of the impossibility of checking whether all we are told is truthful, lying is one of the most important issues in family life. (Ekman, 1989:5)
Example B - Original Text	**Example B - Paraphrase**
"To developmental psychologists, the study of creativity is necessarily anchored in the study of human development." Gardner, H. (1993). *Creating Minds*. New York: Basic Books, p. 31.	Howard Gardner (1993:31) states that psychologists who work in the area of human development think that research into "creativity" must be firmly based in their field of study, developmental psychology. **or** Psychologists who work in the field of human development believe that any research into creativity must be situated firmly in the study of human development (Gardner, 1993:31).

Activity 4   Discussion

1. On your own, read the following and take notes.

   Synonyms tend to replace the original wording of the author. Where synonyms are not available, you may have to use more words than the author wrote to make the idea clear. This is the case with the second paraphrase. Also notice that all of the ideas expressed by the author are used. It is very important when paraphrasing the work of another person that you express the ideas carefully so that they are accurate and not distorted. Be sure that the reader knows whose ideas they are by citing the source. The parenthetical reference includes the author's last name, the year, and the page reference. This refers readers to a reference section that appears at the end of an essay. In the alphabetical reference section, readers would find a complete citation, consisting of the author's name, the title of the publication, the place of publication, and the publisher. This citation is meant to allow interested readers to locate the original source.

2. As a class, discuss the concept of paraphrasing and the use of synonyms, changes in sentence structure, and other means of putting things into your own words with the class.

Activity 5   Suggested Steps for Paraphrasing

As a class, discuss the following steps for paraphrasing:
1. Read the passage carefully.
2. Identify synonyms for the words in the passage.
3. Where synonyms are not available, think of how to change the parts of speech or the sentence structure.
4. If the passage has long sentences, break them up into smaller sentences. If the passage contains short sentences, combine some of the ideas.
5. Write out your paraphrase and then read it carefully. Is the meaning the same as in the original passage? Do you have more than three consecutive words taken from the original passage? If so, this is often considered plagiarism.
6. Check to see if you have cited your source in parenthesis either at the beginning of the paraphrase or at the end.

Activity 6   Vocabulary Development

With a partner, brainstorm as many verbs and phrases as possible that can be used to report what another person has said. Some possible words to use for reported speech, often referred to as *reporting words* are: Black (1990:13) "says"/ "states"/ "concurs"/ "argues"/ "reports" that...; According to Black (1990:13), ...; In Black's (1990:13) view ... Make a list of your verbs and phrases; then compare them with the whole class. Discuss differences in meaning—for example, *concurs* and *argues* are not likely to be interchangeable.

_____ _____ _____

_____ _____ _____

_____ _____ _____

The list developed in this activity will be a useful resource to help you add variety to the way in which you introduce someone else's words.

Activity 7 Paraphrasing

Paraphrase the following statements and use the APA conventions shown in the example text on page 70 to cite the sources. Think carefully about what information you need to include in parenthesis. If necessary, go back to Examples A and B, on page 71.

1. "Picasso's ambivalence toward the work was heightened by the reaction of his acquaintances and friends." This quotation is found on page 139 in *Creating Minds* by Howard Gardner, published in 1993 by Basic Books in New York, N.Y.

_____

_____

_____

_____

2. "They were compelling questions, and the emotional intensity in the parents' voices bespoke a deep concern, and a deeper frustration." Paul Ekman used these words in *Why Kids Lie*, on page 7 which was published in 1989 by Penguin Books in London, England.

_____

_____

_____

_____

3. "I shall make practical suggestions for the classroom, but many people would say that in the reading class it is the teacher's understanding of the reading process that is more important than anything else." This is found in Christine Nuttall's 1982 book, *Teaching Reading Skills in a Foreign Language* on page 1. This book was published by Heinemann International in Oxford.

_____

_____

_____

_____

Paraphrasing is a challenging skill for many writers. Several options are usually available, which is why your instructor will check your answers and show you the best responses from the class.

> **NOTE: Paraphrasing is generally preferred to quotation because it shows that you understand the material. This may be important to the teacher or professor for whom you are writing a paper.**

Revising Your Paraphrase

1. Select one of three statements in Activity 7.
2. Reread the original statement, and then compare it with the paraphrase you wrote in Activity 7.
3. Place a check mark (√) in front of each statement that applies to your paraphrase.
   The paraphrase
   A. includes all the important ideas in the original.
   B. avoids unnecessary or irrelevant ideas.
   C. accurately represents specific and general ideas.
   D. places the same emphasis on the ideas as the original.
   E. uses appropriate vocabulary and effective sentence structure.
   F. contains nothing that might be considered plagiarism.
4. Make any changes necessary to achieve an accurate, well-constructed paraphrase.

2. Plagiarism

Plagiarism is the act of using ideas and words from someone else and passing them off as one's own. As few as three consecutive words taken from someone else's text may be considered an incidence of plagiarism and could result in negative consequences. The consequences tend to depend on the severity of each case and the context. Some possible consequences are a failing grade on the essay concerned, failure in the course, suspension from the institution, or other disciplinary action.

Writers may commit plagiarism deliberately or as a result of poor notetaking skills or sloppy referencing techniques. To avoid plagiarising others, writers need to keep careful documentation of their research. Keeping complete bibliographical information, including page numbers, of each source helps writers acknowledge their sources. When they compose their text, they need to acknowledge ideas, opinions, theories, and facts that are not common knowledge. Phrases and sentences that represent a direct quotation are placed between quotation marks. Paraphrased material is referenced to indicate the source.

How to Avoid Plagiarism

Because plagiarism–the presentation of someone else's words or ideas as your own–is a serious offence, it is important to take steps to avoid it. There are at least three steps necessary to avoid it.
1. Be sure to identify the source of your material. Identify the person whose idea you are using in parenthesis by name at the end of the quotation or paraphrase.
2. If the words are directly taken from the original source, place them in quotation marks or set them out in the method used for a longer quotation (for an example, see "Set-off Quotation" on page 75).
3. If you paraphrase the material, be sure that the way you have expressed the ideas is not too close to the original, as this may also result in plagiarism.

3. Using Quotations

A quotation uses the exact words of another person as they appear in the original material.

Awareness Raising

As a class, discuss the following questions:
1. What is a quotation?
2. Why or when should you quote a source?

If using a summary or a paraphrase takes away from the impact or power of the original, then writers may opt to use a quotation. Writers may add weight to an argument by citing the exact words of an expert in the field, as these words acknowledge the experience and expertise of the person being quoted. In spite of these possible benefits, it is important not to overuse quotations in an essay or paper. If a quotation seems to be the most effective means to make a point, its length needs to be considered carefully. Short quotations are preferable. As well, the number of quotations should be limited. A useful guideline is to keep them to under 10 percent of the entire text. Finally, quotations should be incorporated into the writer's own arguments and sentences. They serve to substantiate the points made in an essay.

Guidelines for the Use of Quotations

Quotations need to reflect the words of the original text accurately, including the original punctuation and capitalisation. A general guideline is that quotations that are less than five typed lines are enclosed in double quotation marks. This is called an in-line quotation.

Example: In-line Quotation

This point is corroborated by Collins (1997:21), who says "personality appears to be stable over time."

For passages that are longer than five typed lines, a set-off style is appropriate. In this case, the quotation is indented by ten spaces from the left margin and is double-spaced. Quotation marks are not necessary for the set-off style.

Example: Set-off Quotation

Earlier in history man was considered the centre of the universe. However, Charles Darwin (1881) forces us to consider our sometimes overinflated view of man when he says

> the plow is one of the most ancient and most valuable of man's inventions; but long before
>
> he existed the land was in fact regularly plowed, and still continues to be thus plowed by
>
> earthworms. It may be doubted whether there are many other animals which have played
>
> so important a part in the history of the world, as have these lowly organised creatures.

This respect for the lowliest creatures of nature has led us to a new emphasis on ecosystems. (cited in Bartlett 1992:444)

If parts of a quotation are left out, such omissions should not change the meaning of the original. They are signalled through spaced periods known as ellipses.

Example: Ellipses

Nanda (1985:133) quotes Ghandi as once saying, "I am an average man with less than an average ability. . . . There is a limit on the development of the intellect but none to that of the heart."
Reference
Nanda, B.R. (1985). *Ghandi and His Critics*. Delhi: Oxford University Press.

Activity 10   Using Quotations in Written Work

1. Choose one of the following topics:.
   - A notable person such as Marie Curie, Amelia Earhart, Albert Einstein, Sigmund Freud, Mahatma Ghandi, Margaret Thatcher
   - Multinational corporations
   - Nationalism or separatism
   - Another topic approved by your teacher
2. Do your research at a library. Go to the library and find two sources (articles or books) on your topic. Read up on your topic.
3. Brainstorm ideas about your topic, using a diagram or list of ideas.
4. Develop a thesis statement and an outline for an essay.
5. Write a rough draft of your essay and compile a reference page for your sources. Incorporate at least two quotations from your sources.
6. Exchange drafts with a peer and discuss the following:
   - the content and organisation of the draft
   - the use of the sources and the way in which they are cited in the text
   - the reference page and its format.
7. Make any changes and edit your work, using the Editing Checklist, page 167. Use the computer or a dictionary to check the spelling.
8. Hand in your work for feedback and evaluation.

4. The Reference Section

All sources used in the body of a text are listed systematically in the reference section at the end of an essay or paper. Reference sections at the end of books, papers, and similar texts are compiled in one of several standard formats. One frequently used standard, APA Style, is used in this text (see Example of a Reference List, page 176). However, when writing an essay to fulfill the requirements of an assignment, writers should check with their professor or department secretary to find out what format is preferred.

Activity 11   Awareness Raising

Return to the beginning of this unit and discuss the following questions with the whole class.
1. What order do the names follow in the reference section?
2. What information is required in each reference?
3. How is each source recorded (order of information, order of names, punctuation)?

Activity 12   Writing a Reference Section

1. Use the sources from the paraphrasing activity (Activity 7) to create a reference section.
2. Check each source carefully to be sure that the information is complete and the format is correct.
3. Write your reference section in the space below or on a computer if you have access to one.

_____

_____

_____

_____

_____

_____

5. Summarising

A summary is a shortened version of a text. It should contain all the essential ideas from the original but without the finer details of the original.

Writing a summary involves reading for the thesis or main idea and major supporting points of the original text. These ideas are then written in your own words. As with paraphrasing, identifying the author and the source of the material summarised is important. This technique may be used as a separate assignment, as in "Write a summary of a recent article on NAFTA." Or it may be combined with a critique of the author's thesis, as in "Discuss Jones's recent article on pollution." In the latter case, you would be required to write a summary of the author's work, then discuss the strength and wisdom of those arguments and any research used to support them. Unlike a paraphrase, which can be the same length as the original or longer, a summary will be shorter than the original. When collecting material for a research paper, students often paraphrase or summarise information on notecards. For more details on using notecards see Real Life Writing Task 7 – The Research Paper. If you use this technique, be sure to take careful note of the reference of each source document you use.

General guidelines apply in summarising a text, although each text will be slightly different and may require a different initial approach.

Guidelines to Writing a Summary

Step 1: Read the article to get the gist or main idea.

Step 2: Underline the thesis. *Hint:* The thesis is usually found in the introduction and/or conclusion of an article, so check there first. But don't forget that rules and patterns can be broken. You may have to look at the title, paragraph topics, and conclusion to decide what the thesis is.

Step 3: Scan each paragraph and underline the topic of the paragraph. *Hint:* The topic is frequently found at the beginning of the paragraph in the topic sentence and may be reiterated in the concluding sentence.

Step 4: Develop a topic sentence that gives the main idea of the original and includes the author's name, the title of the article if needed, and the date of publication.

6. Identifying the Essentials

A summary is likely to be just a fraction of the length of the original, especially if the original text is quite lengthy. Reducing the text of an original to that extent requires a clear sense of what the original is about and what, in the original, is essential. This will require a clear understanding of the thesis or focus and the main points of the original text.

| Activity 13 | Awareness Raising |

Read the text entitled "Stereotypes: Who Works the Hardest?" published in *The Industrial Journal*, September 16, 1997, page 16. Be ready to answer some questions after you have read the text.

Stereotypes: Who Works the Hardest?

Kevan Dadgar

From an early age we develop stereotypes about people from other countries and cultures. Canadians are quiet and peaceful. Latins are passionate and full of fun. The English are studious and boring or perhaps eccentric. Germans are hardworking, industrious people. Asians are shy in class. Of course there is no way that such generalisations could apply to a whole population. These stereotypes break down as we get to know people from a cultural group and recognise the diversity. Sometimes, though, statistics come along to show how wrong our stereotypes are. The notion that Germans work harder than most is one stereotype that has recently fallen into disrepute.

Statistics from the European community show that Germans spend less time than other Europeans on the job. Germans work only 1697 hours on average. This was the lowest total in the EC. This is the equivalent of 212 eight-hour days or 60% of the days in a year on the job. The French, Italians, and British put in 1767, 1768, and 1778 in that order. Spanish workers spend 1800 hours while the Greeks and Irish are in the mid-1800's. Portuguese workers spend the longest hours at work, more than 2100 hours a year. North Americans spend more time at work than the average European and the Japanese work even longer hours than the Portuguese. How is it that the Germans are the winners in the amount of leisure time they have?

There are several factors that contribute to this. First, they have powerful unions. They made shorter working hours their top demand in labour negotiations. Companies in Germany acceded to the demands and the average work week now is about 35 hours a week. Working on Saturday and Sunday is almost unheard of in German industry, and most employees are entitled to vacations of six weeks a year with extra time allowed for training and illness. On top of this, there are more national holidays than in many countries. In most German states there are ten official holidays. These statistics illustrate the reality that the workers in Germany have more legal holiday time than most other nations.

Until recent times, the Protestant work ethic drove the workforce in Germany. However, as the popular song says, "The times they are a-changin." It appears that growing numbers of German workers are taking time off for "illness." In government offices absenteeism has been known to reach 30% on Mondays. This indicates that malingering is becoming common and attitudes to work may be changing. With all this free time, what do these workers do? Mostly they travel. It is not unusual to see German tourists taking long holidays in distant lands. Obviously, the employers are not keen on the workers having all this paid leisure time. Some believe that it may contribute to a loss of competitiveness in the world market. The unions' hope was that as the workers' hours became shorter the companies would be forced to hire more workers. However, management have introduced labour-saving techniques and flex hours so that in spite of the shorter hours, production and production costs have not been directly affected. They may not be working such long hours but they are working hard. What does that say about the stereotype? It may depend on how you measure "hardworking" and "industrious."

Activity 14 | Important Information

List the information that may be needed to write your summary.

The author: _____ The title:_____

The year of publication: _____ The journal: _____

_____

The author's thesis: _____

_____

_____

Main supporting points:_____

_____

_____

A possible topic sentence:_____

_____

_____

Comparing your findings with those of a peer helps you clarify your own ideas. It should also allow you to decide whether you have left out any important information or misinterpreted any of the original writer's ideas.

Activity 15   **Comparing Findings**

1. Work with a partner to compare your notes. Discuss any differences you may find.
2. Go back to the original text if you are uncertain about some points, then make any changes needed.

Once you have reviewed your material, you are ready to write a first draft of your summary.

Activity 16   **Writing a Draft**

Write a one-paragraph summary of the article. Remember to create a topic sentence, put the ideas into your own words, and be sure that you make it clear that you reflect the author's ideas, not your own.

Activity 17   **Reviewing the Summary**

Work with a partner you have not worked with recently.
1. Review your summary and consider the questions below.
2. Make a note of suggested changes or improvements.
   A. Does the topic sentence identify the source?
   B. Are the main supporting points included? Are they in order?
   C. Is the writing clear?
   D. Is there an effective concluding sentence?

Any changes the partner suggested should be marked on the draft to enable the writer of the summary to consider them later. Thinking about these suggestions is important for writers; writers need to determine whether to incorporate the suggestions in their revised summary.

Activity 18   **Editing the Summary**

1. Edit your summary using the Editing Checklist, page167, looking especially for errors that you often make.
2. Make changes or rewrite if necessary, and then hand in your summary for feedback from your instructor.

Summary of Unit 6

In this unit you
- worked on paraphrasing, quoting sources, and citing the sources you paraphrased or quoted
- practised using the format for a reference section
- became aware of how to avoid plagiarism
- practised writing a summary of a short essay.

Alternate or Additional Activities

1. Copy a sentence from a reading that you have prepared recently. Give all the information needed for a reference section. Exchange your sentence with a classmate. Paraphrase your classmate's sentence and use parenthetical references in your paraphrase. Write out the reference information in the format required for a reference section.

2. Each day, for an entire week, your instructor will give you a sentence to paraphrase. You will have ten minutes to rewrite the ideas expressed in the sentence in your own words. Alternately, the class as a whole can complete the paraphrase together on the board.

3. Each day, two of your peers will be selected to present a paraphrase of something they read the day before in the newspaper, using indirect speech. Pay careful attention to the reporting verbs (see page 72) they use. Add them to your list (Activity 6) if you do not have them listed already.

4. Look up a quotation by a past or present leader from your home country. You can do this on the Internet or you can choose a recent news article. Write a short paragraph, either giving your opinion of what the person said or explaining it. Share this paragraph with your classmates before presenting it to your instructor for feedback and evaluation.

5. Find a short article in a newspaper or magazine on a topic that interests you. Write a summary of the article in one paragraph.

6. Summarise a paragraph or essay that you have written.

REAL LIFE WRITING
THE ESSAY

Task 1 | REAL LIFE WRITING THE ESSAY

 Objectives: - To expand the development of a topic from paragraph to essay
- To practise introductory and concluding paragraphs
- To write an essay comparing two ideas or objects

The focus of this task is on writing a multi-paragraph essay, incorporating several of the techniques practised in earlier units. The main task in this unit consists of writing a multi-paragraph comparison-and-contrast essay. The type of writing presented in this unit can be applied to many different writing requirements in academic and professional settings.

1. Review

The paragraph on Niagara Falls introduced in Unit 2, reproduced below, includes four supporting sentences, in addition to the introductory and concluding sentences. Each of these supporting sentences could serve as the topic sentence for a paragraph, in which the ideas expressed would be expanded.

Activity 1   Awareness Raising

Read the paragraph on Niagara Falls. Then think about how you might expand on the ideas by including more details in each one. You may wish to develop your ideas about another city, one that you know well. Go back to Unit 2 to remind yourself of how a single-paragraph text relates to a multi-paragraph text.

Niagara Falls
François Bélanger

Niagara Falls attracts a wide variety of visitors all year round. Each winter, tourists enjoy looking at the iced-up falls and the colourful Festival of Lights. In the spring, they come to admire the cascades of water from melted ice that tumble over the falls and the blossoms in the nearby peach and cherry orchards. During the summer months, tourists delight in watching the falls, maybe from one of the tour boats, and the falling water which produces sprays of mist that drench unsuspecting tourists and create rainbows above them. In the fall, visitors like to combine their visit to the falls with a tour of the fall foliage. The change of the seasons may alter the way the falls look, but the views are always stunning.

Activity 2   Brainstorming Supporting Ideas

In the spaces below, write down your additional supporting ideas for each of the four sentences. In small groups or with the entire class, discuss your ideas, and then draft four additional paragraphs.

1. Each winter: _____

_____

2. In the spring: _____

_____

3. During the summer: _____

_____

4. In the fall: _____

_____

The topic sentence and concluding sentence from the original paragraph on Niagara Falls will not serve your expanded text adequately; they need to be revised. Each of the two sentences should be expanded to form a paragraph.

The first paragraph of an essay serves as an introduction to the topic. It should use some way to catch the reader's interest, include the thesis statement, and signal to readers how this thesis will be developed. Some possible ways to make an introduction appealing are using a brief story, using a surprising fact, using statistics, using a relevant quotation, or giving some historical background. Think carefully about the audience you are writing for, as you want to choose something that will catch their interest. Usually the thesis statement comes at the end of the introduction. Therefore, the transition from your interest catcher to your thesis should be smooth and logical.

The concluding paragraph leaves a final and important impression on your reader. It often summarises in a few words what you have said in the essay without repeating it exactly. In this way, it refers back to the thesis statement and affirms it. Other techniques writers use in conclusions are proposing a solution, making a prediction, or making a recommendation. Again your purpose, audience, and topic will influence your choice. As you read through the sample essay on Niagara Falls below, note how the writer has evoked the readers' interest in the introduction and tried to make the concluding paragraph leave a good final impression.

| Activity 3 | Introductory and Concluding Paragraphs |

In small groups
1. Discuss ways in which you might develop your introductory and concluding paragraphs. As this process will depend on the ideas you decided to include in each of the four paragraphs, there are several possibilities.

On your own, and before you read the sample essay,
2. Brainstorm some ideas and write them in the spaces provided.
3. Read the sample essay on Niagara Falls.
4. Compare the techniques you have used to catch the readers' interest and conclude your essay.

Introductory Paragraph

"Niagara Falls (or a city of your choice) attracts a wide variety of visitors all year round."

Topic sentence: _____

Signalling development: _____

Thesis statement: _____

Concluding Paragraph

Topic sentence: _____

Summarising ideas: _____

Concluding sentence: _____

Here is one person's example for expanding the paragraph about Niagara Falls into an essay.

Niagara Falls

Planning a trip to Niagara Falls involves making decisions about a number of things, for instance where to stay, whom to go with, and what to pack. A key decision is when to take the trip. Deciding when to visit Niagara Falls is not easy because every season offers some advantages.

In winter, despite the cold, Niagara Falls is a wonderland. The snow turns it into a vision in white. Because of the cold, the mist encrusts the trees, the lampposts, and virtually everything in a layer of ice. Everything gleams and sparkles in sunlight and lamplight, making magic images for photographers. The ice begins to cover the river and perhaps makes a bridge across the water. If it is very cold, the ice snaps and crackles, entertaining visitors. Finally, if you like to have a tourist attraction to yourself or just hate crowds and line-ups, winter is the time to go. The cold and the fact that some attractions may be closed are hardly noticed when you are viewing such beauty.

Spring will also capture your heart in Niagara. The lawns and hills in the park by the falls are covered in daffodils. In the flowerbeds, pansies and tulips and spring perennials wave in the gentle wind. If you make it in May, the surrounding countryside is dotted with farms full of fruit trees in blossoms of pink and white. Birders enjoy the large variety of species that migrate through the area. Lastly, the temperature and the crowds are moderate, and that makes walking and sightseeing less tiring.

Most people choose summer to visit the falls. It may be because that is holiday time and the weather is more predictably pleasant. There is the stimulation of crowds of people from many lands dressed in a variety of costumes. The perennial flowerbeds and rose gardens are in full bloom. Also all of the sites and attractions are operating when you holiday in peak season. The best ride of all, the Maid of the Mist, shuttles up close to the falls and that is my favourite ride. Summer guarantees warmth and sunshine and many rainbows, so it is no wonder that it is a popular time to visit.

Lastly, fall offers its own particular joys. The trees on the escarpment change to red and gold with dashes of orange and of course the green of firs. The weather is usually cool but sunny and dry, perfect for hiking the many trails or cycling on the bicycle path that extends the length of the Niagara River from Niagara-on-the-Lake to Fort Erie. There are fewer people and that means better and quicker service and fewer line-ups. Fall has much to commend itself to tourists in the region.

Listing the advantages of each season is one way to help you decide when to take a trip. This could make decisionmaking easier for some destinations. However, Niagara Falls appears to be a place for all seasons. If you are a photographer, you will not want to miss any season. You may decide to go once a year and check out each season before you can say which you like best.

Activity 4 | Reviewing Organisation and Outlining

With a partner, fill in the following outline for the sample essay on Niagara Falls.

I–Introduction: _____

_____

Thesis Statement: _____

II–Body Paragraph 1
Topic: _____

_____

_____

_____

III–Body Paragraph 2
Topic: _____

_____

_____

_____

IV–Body Paragraph 3
Topic: _____

_____

_____

_____

_____

_____

_____

V–Body Paragraph 4

Topic: _____

_____

_____

_____

VI–Conclusion

_____

_____

_____

_____

2. Comparison/Contrast Essay Writing

Apply the techniques for paragraph development discussed in the previous section to develop a comparison-and-contrast essay. You may wish to review Unit 4, on basic principles for comparison-contrast writing, before you continue with this task. You will need to choose between block and alternating styles. If necessary, review the discussion of these two styles in Unit 4, pages 47-48; also, look at the style of the Outline Examples 1 and 2 below. As shown above, the first paragraph in academic writing usually presents an introduction to the topic. Typically, this paragraph develops from more general ideas about the topic to a very specific thesis statement. The introduction is like a lure used to catch a fish; it should attract the reader to "bite"–to continue reading. The thesis statement signals the intentions of the writer to the reader; it introduces the narrowed topic, states the opinion or intention, and predicts how the body of the essay will be organised. The last paragraph usually restates the thesis and then offers a concluding statement, which should leave the reader feeling satisfied with the ideas presented.

Outline Example One (Alternating/Point by Point Method)
  I–Introduction
   Topic: Cars–difficult decision–most important criteria for choosing
   Thesis Statement: Although Car A and Car B are similar in terms of size and price, the level of owner satisfaction causes me to prefer Car B.
  II–Body Paragraph 1
   Topic: size–similar
   Seats 5
   Small trunk
   Easy to park
   Light–therefore has low gas mileage

III–Body Paragraph

Topic: price–similar

Quote prices–what is included with each

IV–Body Paragraph 3

Topic: level of owner satisfaction–different

Reasons owners give for satisfaction

V–Conclusion

Both good cars–give ratings

Restate thesis

However, since so close in so many ways, I'd buy whichever was cheapest.

Example Two (Block Comparison)

I–Introduction

Topic: Cars–difficult decision–what most important criteria

Thesis statement: Though there are some differences, their many similarities give both Car A and Car B excellent value in a car.

II–Topic: Differences

Reports of owner satisfaction–report statistics

Price–Car A a bit higher, though not much–give data

III–Topic: Similarities

Size–give data from sales leaflet

Gas Economy–as above

Options

IV–Conclusion:

Personal experience with Car B–satisfied

Restate thesis–so I would buy either if I could get a bargain.

NOTE: Lemon-Aid book–buyer's guide. Lemon-Aid by Phil Edmonston is published regularly (by Stoddart) in North America to inform consumers of performance records of cars. Related information is available at http://www.lemonaidcars.com/home.htm

---

Activity 5   Reading

1. Read the following sample essays, paying particular attention to how they develop the ideas.
2. Be prepared to identify outline patterns for the sample essays.

Sample Essay 1: Freud and Jung: A Brief Comparison

Vlasta Subic

Two of the most influential people in the psychoanalytic movement of the early 1900s were Freud and Jung. Having begun a friendship in a letter exchange, they became close friends and associates. However, all this changed as Jung's thinking evolved. Their paths divided and their close friendship ended. Obviously, personality and rivalry could have influenced this rift. On the other hand, a brief examination of Freud's and Jung's theories indicates that substantial differences in their ideas formed the basis of that break.

Freud's system of the psyche included the concepts of the id, ego, and superego. The id is made up of the inherited instinctive impulses of the individual and is part of the unconscious. The ego is the part of the mind that mediates between the id and the superego and deals with external reality. The superego is that part of the mind that acts as a conscience and responds to social rules. These concepts and a series of psychosexual stages form a basis for Freud's thought. Another emphasis in Freud's ideas is the role of sex in the development of the psyche and resulting behaviour. This sexual conduct he saw as present even in the infant. The Oedipus theory of Freud, for example, said that boys develop a deep emotional attachment of a sexual nature to their mothers and become jealous of their fathers, which leads to a strong hatred toward the father that is then sublimated by imitating and idealising him. Finally, Freud viewed the unconscious as the repository of repressed memories, especially of sexual trauma, and thought this was the basis for all neuroses. An overview of Jung's theory exposes how different their thinking was.

Unlike Freud's, Jung's basic theory looks at the concepts of introversion and extroversion and the four psychological functions of sensation, intuition, thinking, and feeling. These concepts are expanded into a complex view of different personality types. Our basic personality affects the way we behave. Thus there is a basic difference in the concepts that the two use to explain behaviour. Secondly, and a major influence in their disagreement, is that Jung disagreed with Freud's emphasis on sexual trauma as the basis for all neurosis. He disagreed with the Oedipus theory of Freud. Jung de-emphasised the role of sex in his theories. In addition, whereas Freud saw the unconscious as a storehouse of repressed memories, Carl Jung, influenced by Eastern tradition and thought, asserted that the unconscious encompassed both the personal and the collective unconscious. The latter he saw as shaped by what he calls archetypes, such as self, anima/animus, and persona. Jung asserted that every individual has a common pool of memories, almost like a genetic knowledge that is the same for all humans. Whereas Freud explained the idealisation of fathers by sons using the Oedipus theory, Jung saw the forces that led to idealisation of fathers by sons to be part of this collective unconscious. Jung, as can be seen, had many basic disagreements in theory with Freud.

Although Jung and Freud were in agreement early in Jung's career, a brief examination of their theories shows that they veered away from each other in their thoughts. This exhibited itself in their theories of personality and psychoanalysis in many ways. The above are just one or two such conflicts. Both now have their opponents and supporters. Another one hundred years and perhaps our understanding of the human psyche may unravel the puzzle of who is right. Then again the mind and hearts of humans may be so complex as to make this task impossible or it may prove that somehow both were right.

Sample Essay 2: Restaurant Choice

Pierre Bouchard

Eating out is becoming the great Canadian pastime. In recent years, Greek food has become very popular and there are many new Greek restaurants in our area. Athena and Tellos are two well-known Greek restaurants in Toronto. Both of these restaurants are medium sized and inexpensive. Although they are similar, the differences in environment and variety of food lead me to prefer Tellos.

The environments are quite different in these two restaurants. Tellos has a very romantic setting. Every table has candles. There is lots of space between the tables and many little alcoves so you can have private conversations. There are even three special tables set in alcoves with beaded curtains for total privacy. On the other hand, Athena is very crowded. The tables are close together. The lights are bright and the kitchen is open and noisy. It appeals to large numbers of families with children who run around and make noise. Married couples with families prefer Athena because there is no need to worry about children and their noise and if I get married perhaps I will prefer it. But Tellos is a wonderful place to go with my girlfriend and for now I prefer the environment there.

Tellos is preferable for me also because of the variety of choices on the menu. The menu contains about twenty different kinds of appetizers such as flaming cheese, which is an exciting choice. There are always at least four daily specials and a menu with many other choices. Athena, by contrast, has a set menu of appetizers and three entrees and only one special of the day. Trying something different every visit makes a restaurant more interesting for me and that's why Tellos is my choice.

Although they are very similar in cost and about the same size, the wider choice and warm, quiet atmosphere at Tellos make it more inviting for me. You will get a great meal at both restaurants and both are a bargain. If, like me, you want to impress a girl, or if you plan to ask her to marry you, do not go to Athena. Instead, go to Tellos because you will find the exciting cheese flambé and the romantic candlelight and music a perfect setting for that special date.

| Activity 6 | Outline for Sample Essay 1 |

Below,
1. Fill in the outline for Sample Essay 1.
2. Then compare your outline with outlines prepared by two peers.
3. Finally, discuss any differences you may find with your peers.

I–Introduction: _____

_____

Thesis Statement: _____

II–Body Paragraph 1

Topic: _____

_____

_____

_____

III–Body Paragraph 2

Topic: _____

_____

_____

_____

IV–Conclusion

_____

_____

_____

_____

Activity 7   **Outline for Sample Essay 2**

Below,

    1. Fill in the outline for Sample Essay 2.

    2. Then compare your outline with outlines prepared by two peers.

    3. Discuss any differences you may find.

I–Introduction

_____

_____

Thesis Statement: _____

II–Body Paragraph 1

Topic: _____

_____

III–Body Paragraph 2

Topic: _____

_____

_____

IV–Conclusion

_____

_____

Activity 8   Selecting a Topic

Select a topic for comparison from one of the following, or write about any topic of your choice that has been accepted by your instructor.

Two teachers   Two singers   Two different career paths

Two movies   Two actors   Wedding customs in two countries

Two governments   Two political leaders   Two forms of entertainment

Activity 9   Brainstorming Ideas

1. Use the diagram below to generate ideas about your topic.
2. Draw additional lines to write as many characteristics and other ideas as you can about each of the two aspects you want to compare.

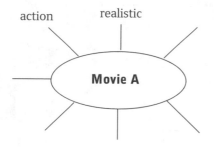

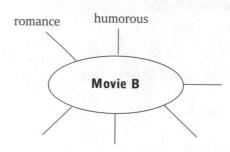

Activity 10   Getting Ready to Write

Think about the PAT Principle (see Unit 1, pages 4-6): Answer the following questions.
    1. What is your purpose for your essay (e.g., to inform, to challenge, to amuse the reader).

_____

_____

_____

2. Do you need to narrow your topic? If so, what is your narrowed topic?

_____

_____

_____

3. What is your opinion or point of view about the topic?

_____

_____

4. Will you use block or point-by-point arrangement of ideas in the essay?

_____

5. Which categories of comparison do you intend to discuss?

_____

6. Write two or three possible thesis statements for your essay.

_____

_____

_____

Activity 11 Developing an Outline for Your Essay

Make an informal point-form outline for your essay in the space below.

Thesis Statement: _____

I–Introduction

Topic: _____

_____

_____

III–Body Paragraph 2

Topic: _____

_____

_____

II–Body Paragraph 1   IV–Conclusion

Topic: _____   _____

_____   _____

Activity 12 | Writing the First Draft

1. With a peer or your instructor, discuss the thesis statement, the points you intend to make, and the points and illustrations in your outline.
2. Think about the order of your ideas and how the thesis predicts the order of the paragraphs.
3. Make any changes that are necessary in your outline.
4. Now write a rough draft of your essay, using your outline.

Activity 13 | Peer Feedback

Follow the directions carefully in this activity. You will be asked to answer some questions before you continue reading your peers' work.
1. Meet with one or two other students.
2. Exchange your papers and answer the questions below.
3. Write your answers and comments on a separate sheet of paper that you can give to the author.
Read your peer's introduction.
A. What technique does the author use in the introduction to get the reader's interest?
B. What is the thesis statement?
C. Answer this question before you read on: What do you think the topics for the body paragraphs will be?
Read the rest of the essay.
D. Did the body paragraphs meet your expectations? Explain.
E. Are the body paragraphs well-organised and logical?
F. What information do you find unclear?
G. What techniques did the author use to conclude the essay?
H. What did you like best about the essay?
I. What suggestions do you have to improve it?

Activity 14 | Self-Evaluation and Editing

1. Reread your essay and think about suggestions you received from your classmate(s) or instructor.
2. Decide on what changes you need to make to improve the content and organisation.
3. Check that the content requirements as given by your instructor have been met: have you written the assigned number of words and paragraphs?
4. Make the suggested changes, and then follow the suggestions in the editing guide below.

Editing Guide

Place a check mark (√) on the line when you have completed each step.
____ If you use a computer, do a spell check.
____ If your paper is handwritten, check your spelling by using a dictionary.
____ Check your paper, one sentence at the time, looking for grammatical errors. Try to develop an

awareness of mistakes you make frequently and watch out for them.

___ Look for run-on or incomplete sentences.

___ Use the Editing Checklist in the Resource Centre, pages 167-168.

___ Check the formatting. Did you follow the requirements as specified by your instructor?

___ Hand in your paper for evaluation and feedback from your instructor.

Summary of Real Life Writing Task 1

In this task you
- reviewed a descriptive paragraph
- explored how its supporting sentences may serve as topic sentences for separate paragraphs in an essay
- developed introductory and concluding paragraphs
- practised these techniques by writing a comparison/contrast essay, going through the steps of outlining, topic development, drafting, peer feedback, revising, and editing.

Alternate or Additional Assignments

1. Use the paragraph on Niagara Falls as a model to develop a descriptive essay about a place, person, or object you know well. Write for an audience unfamiliar with the place, person, or object. Your purpose might be to encourage your audience to visit the place or to get to know the person or object you describe.

2. Use the Internet to research two major industrial cities and the benefits each offers to attract new companies. Write a comparison/contrast essay as a preliminary source of information for the board of directors of a company of your choice.

3. Describe, and then compare the different options the education system in your country offers its students. Your audience might be peers in your class who are not familiar with the education system in your country, peers you wish to inform, or parents who wish to make informed choices for their children's schooling. As a follow up, work with a peer from a different country and compare the systems described in your essays.

REAL LIFE WRITING
ANSWERING QUESTIONS

Task 2

REAL LIFE WRITING
ANSWERING QUESTIONS

Objectives: -To practise answering questions through:
-analysis of what the question is about and what kind of information is requested
-identification of the focus of the question
-planning and writing a focussed response (with a main point, idea, topic sentence, thesis)
-developing examples or supporting documentation to support your response
-learning to deal with time limits

Different types of questions are used on language tests and other types of examinations. Successful answers to these questions require an ability to analyse the question to determine what information is expected.

Activity 1 | Awareness Raising

1. What types of test do you find most difficult?
2. What makes these tests difficult?
3. What strategies do you use to help you succeed on a test?

1. Short-Answer and Essay Questions

Short-answer and essay questions require similar answering techniques. The main difference between them is that the first is usually limited to one paragraph. Questions that require short answers, typically one paragraph in length, are frequently used to test students' ability to define a term, explain a process or concept, or compare two or more ideas. They also test students' ability to analyse the question, and to organise and support their ideas.

Analysing the Question

Before you can begin to answer the question, you need to understand it. Read questions twice to help you understand what you are asked to do. Questions are typically in the imperative form, giving directions or instructions that begin with a verb that tells you what you need to do. Words typically used include those found on the list below. Each word signals an appropriate kind of response:

a) *describe, discuss, review,* or *state*
   suggest that you should tell all you know about the topic;

b) *compare, contrast, explain, define, diagram,* or *illustrate*
   indicate that you should focus on certain specific characteristics or certain limited facts and explain them to the reader; the first two words indicate that there are two or more items or ideas involved;

c) *enumerate, list, summarise, outline, tabulate,* or *trace*
   likely expect you to give important facts and a brief example for each to show that you understand a concept or point (sometimes the marking scheme may suggest that more detail is required);

d) *evaluate, interpret,* or *justify*
   express an interest in your own opinion and expect you to show how well you can substantiate your opinion;

e) *analyse, criticise,* or *select*
   suggest that you should break a specific component into smaller parts.

Identifying the Focus of a Question

The question likely indicates the focus of the question and reveals what information is required.

Activity 2 **Understanding the Focus of a Question**

1. Read questions a), b), and c) below. Decide what each question asks you to do.
2. Write down your answers.
3. Work with two or three partners to compare your answers.
4. Discuss differences to determine what would be the best approach.

a) What is Confucianism? _____

_____

_____

b) State two main tenets of Confucianism. _____

_____

_____

c) Explain the difference between Confucianism and Individualism.

_____

_____

_____

_____

When you understand the question and the information that its answer requires, try to develop a topic sentence that includes the focus of the question. This strategy will help you stay focussed on what is needed to answer the question. Think about the paragraph pattern that might be most appropriate to answer the question. For example, question a) in Activity 2 above might use the paragraph pattern of Definitions discussed in Unit 3 and could start as follows:

a) Confucianism is.....Definitions discussed in Unit 3

An answer to question b) above might use the paragraph pattern of Description and start as follows:

b) Two main principles of Confucianism are (....) and (....)

The third question in Activity 2, question c) could start like this:

c) Confucianism and Individualism both deal with values held in societies, but Confucianism stresses focus on social groups while Individualism stresses focus on the individual.

This answer would then follow the comparison and contrast paragraph pattern discussed in Unit 4.

Individually,
1. Analyse questions a) through f) below.
2. Determine the required information.
3. Write a topic sentence for each.
4. Suggest an appropriate paragraph pattern.

In small groups or as a class,
5. Compare your answers and discuss differences.
   a) What new words have computers introduced into the English language?
   b) Discuss the advantages and disadvantages of shipping goods by train.
   c) Give an example of commercialism.
   d) Explain the purpose of the World Trade Organisation.
   e) What should be done to stop world hunger?
   f) How is cheese made?

Planning and Writing a Focussed Response

Topic sentences need to be followed up with main and supporting ideas.

Activity 4   **Brainstorming a Response**

Take a few minutes to think about the following questions. Then look at the example about computers below:
1. How will you limit your topic?
2. What main ideas do you want to include?
3. How will you illustrate or support your main idea?
4. Can you develop your topic by combining it with your main ideas?
5. How will you formulate your conclusion?

Question a) in Activity 3 above
"What new words have computers introduced into the English language?"
might be developed as follows:
- Main idea: many new words have entered the English language over the past few years
   a) Some add meaning to an existing meaning.
   b) Some new words have been coined.
   c) Some new word combinations have been formed.
- Supporting ideas: examples
   a) *browser, cache, cookie, surfing*
   b) *emoticon, newbie*
   c) *hyperlink, freeware, multitasking*
- Conclusion: many examples, new ones being added as computer use expands

Computers and New Words: A Sample Response

   Many new words and new word meanings have been introduced into the English language through the use of computers. These new words and word meanings have come about in different ways. Some of these words are completely new words, some use existing words in new combinations, some use existing words and give them additional, new meanings. A first example is the coinage of new words such as *emoticon* and *newbie*. These words are not found in a standard dictionary as they were coined specifically to express meanings related to computers. They sound like English words because they use parts of existing words. *Emot-* is found in *emotion*, *-con* is in words like *lexicon*. By contrast, words like *free* and *ware* or *hyper-* and *link* are found in standard English dictionaries but are now combined into new words like *freeware* and *hyperlink*. These new combinations have computer-related meanings. Finally, words like *cookie, surfing*, and *browser* are words that exist in the English language. These words have traditional meanings unrelated to computing, in addition to new, computer-related meanings. As the use of computers spreads, the English language will likely see many additional new words and new word meanings.

Note how the underlined expressions provide transitions that help link the ideas expressed.

Activity 5   Writing a Response

1. Select three or four of the questions given in Activity 3 above.
2. Identify main and supporting ideas.
3. Develop two of the questions you worked with in step 2 of this activity in separate paragraphs, each with a topic and concluding sentence. Choose whether to adjust the topic sentence you wrote in Activity 3 (3) or to compose a new one.
4. Check your paragraphs and add transitions where appropriate to link your ideas.
5. Discuss your paragraphs with peers who selected the same questions.
6. Revise your paragraphs if necessary and hand them in to your instructor.

Essay questions are analysed in the same way as short-answer questions. However, essay questions need to be developed in more detail, with introductory and concluding paragraphs. Each main idea forms a paragraph, and each paragraph requires supporting ideas. Your instructor will let you know which question you should develop into an essay. Alternately, you can select one of the topics in Activity 6.

Activity 6   Answering an Essay Question

Write an essay on one of the topics listed below:
  a) Describe the writing process.
  b) Discuss the main effects of advertising on consumers.
  c) Has credit buying affected your way of life? Explain.
  d) Do you believe that violence in movies and television programs leads to violence in our society?
  e) Should prostitution be legalised? Explain.
  f) Compare the benefits of a democracy with those of a monarchy.
  g) Should women in the military services be assigned combat duties? Discuss.
  h) What are the main differences between stocks and bonds?

Your teacher may ask you to write an essay on one of the topics in a) – d) as a homework practice assignment. This assignment helps you prepare for a simulated in-class test on one of the topics in e) – h).

2. Fill-in-the-Gap, Multiple-Choice, and Sentence-Completion Questions

Fill-in-the gap and sentence-completion questions test your vocabulary and your understanding of the relationships among the words in a sentence. Knowledge of the situation and of the subject matter may also be necessary. This type of question typically asks you to choose the word that best fits the gap or completes the sentence. Here is an example of a typical question:

> **Sample Question 1**
> Although the students had been late for class, the teacher dismissed them _____ at 15:00 hrs.
> > a) arbitrarily
> > b) one by one
> > c) promptly
> > d) clearly
> > e) eager

Activity 7   Selecting an Answer

Individually,
1. Decide which one of the five options in Sample Question 1 is the best choice.
2. Identify why each of the other four options is a less likely choice.
3. Discuss your answers with your class.

Some fill-in-the-gap tests take the form of a paragraph or more of continuous text. However, many others and most multiple-choice and sentence-completion questions are presented out of context, giving little information about the topic, as shown in Sample Question 1 above. For many of these, the technique of eliminating unlikely choices is very helpful. For example, try to complete Sample Question 2 below. Then practise answering this type of question in Activity 8 below.

> **Sample Question 2**
> _____ business transactions require the cooperation of many different employees in a company.
> > a) Of all
> > b) They are all
> > c) All
> > d) Why are all

Activity 8   Applying the Process of Elimination

Work with two peers to
1. Identify the best answer for the question above.
2. Explain why the other options given are unsuitable answers.
3. Follow the same process with Sample Question 3 below.

Sample Question 3

A medical emergency is a sudden or unexpected condition _____ immediate care to prevent death or serious harm.

  a) it requires
  b) to require
  c) that requires
  d) a requirement of

| **Activity 9** | **Sample Multiple-Choice Questions from an Undergraduate Exam** |

In small groups, use the process of elimination to find the correct answer for the following two questions:

1. The organisation of meaning expressed in a language is referred to as
   a) cognitive organisation
   b) semantic organisation
   c) the lexicon
   d) the grammar

2. When children produce anaphoric reference, they learned how to use
   a) pronouns
   b) adjectives
   c) determiners
   d) syllables

   to maintain reference to previously mentioned characters.

STRATEGIES to answer fill-in-the-gap, multiple-choice, and sentence-completion questions:

- Read the entire sentence first.
- Analyse what type of word might be needed.
- Look for clues that might help you identify the part of speech of the missing word (e.g., noun, pronoun, verb, adverb, or adjective). In Sample Question 1 above, for example, the missing word must be an adverb modifying the verb dismissed.
- Follow a process of elimination: try each answer choice and cross it out if it does not make sense or fit grammatically.
- Watch out for words that show relationships such as contrast (*although, but, despite, however*), sequence (*and, and then, besides, finally, moreover*), comparison (*also, likewise, similarly*). The word *although* in the above question is a clue that the correct word will indicate a contrast to the idea of the students being late for class.

---

3. Learning to Deal with Time Limits

Familiarise yourself with the format of the test. If you are writing a standardised test such as the TOEFL, GRE, or GMAT, download practice material from the Internet, or borrow guides from the library, a bookstore, or a peer. If you are preparing for a class test, ask the instructor if copies of previous examinations are available or ask for details about the format. Knowing the length and time limit of a test helps you understand the pace at which you need to work to complete the test. Knowing the format of a test helps you prepare for the technique(s) necessary to answer the type of questions offered.

Divide the time available over the value of each question. Questions worth more points are likely to need more time for an answer. For example, if you have ninety minutes to answer ten questions, and each one is worth ten points, allow yourself no more than eight minutes for each question.

4. Tips on How to Answer Questions

Before a test or examination
- Learn as much as you can about the type of tasks you will encounter. Ask your instructor what format a test or examination will have and find out whether you can look at a previous version.
- For a standardised test or examination (e.g., the TOEFL, TOEIC, GRE), use practice material and try as many samples as you can before you write the test.

At the beginning of a test or examination
- Before you start to write an examination, read the entire script quickly to give you a sense of what you will need to do.
- Look at all the questions and their point values. Questions that are worth more points (or a higher percentage of the mark) need to be given more time.
- If permitted, answer questions you consider easy first, but note that some tests require you to complete test items in sequence.
- Read the instructions you receive and concentrate on what they ask you to do. Give your opinion only if asked to do so. Follow the instructions carefully. For example, if you are requested to use a pencil, do not use a pen (test sheets may be electronically marked; a computer may not be able to read pen).
- Take time to think and make notes before you start to write your answers. The process of taking notes helps you to organise your ideas and saves time later. Notes, and maybe an outline, will help you write without having to worry about forgetting what you were going to say.
- If you are working on a short-answer question, start with a topic sentence that addresses the question asked. If the question requires an essay, formulate a thesis statement. Incorporate part of the question into the topic sentence or thesis to help you keep to the topic.
- Develop your answer by supporting your main idea with relevant main ideas and important supporting details that you remember from your readings.
- Stay on topic. Do not stray from the topic to write something you know rather than what the question requires. If you find a question difficult to answer, write something, and then move on to the next question without losing time.
- Use the format required. Most exams require full sentences developed into paragraphs rather than numbered lists of individual points. Use the latter only if you run out of time. If the exam requires an essay, organise the different points into paragraphs.
- Complete all the questions. If you are not sure about an answer, especially on fill-in-the-blank and multiple choice tests, take a guess based on your analysis.

NOTE: On some tests, points are deducted for incorrect answers. Where this is the case, random guessing can harm your score. If you can eliminate one or two of the answer options, your chance of choosing the correct answer is increased.

Summary of Real Life Writing Task 2

In this task you

-analysed test and exam questions to determine their focus

-developed answers that gave appropriate supporting details

-examined techniques to deal with time constraints

-looked at test-taking strategies.

REAL LIFE WRITING
THE ANNOTATED BIBLIOGRAPHY

Objectives: - To compile a bibliography
- To write annotations
- To apply and reinforce summarising and referencing skills practised in Unit 6

1. Characteristics of an Annotated Bibliography

An annotated bibliography is a list of sources or citations with a brief note (annotation) about each source listed. Each source gives the precise information necessary to locate the material, as shown in Unit 6. Annotations are notes of varying length that describe, explain, or evaluate the contents of each source listed.

Activity 1   Awareness Raising and Review

1. What is the purpose of a list of references? Think about your answer and take notes.
2. When would it be useful to have an annotated bibliography?
3. Discuss your notes with two or three partners and listen to the points they note.

Note that a bibliography differs from the list of references discussed in Unit 6. It is different because a bibliography lists sources related to a specific topic, while a list of references contains all the sources that are quoted or paraphrased in the body of a document. A bibliography, whether annotated or not, may focus on a few key sources or may provide an exhaustive list, possibly an entire book, of relevant sources, depending on its purpose.

Basic annotations may be primarily descriptive, similar to abstracts found at the beginning of scholarly journal articles or in periodical indexes. More comprehensive annotations include critical analysis, which reveals an author's
- point of view,
- clarity and appropriateness of expression, and
- authority, i.e., the qualifications and experience an author has to speak on the subject.

Annotations for university and college assignments often include specific requirements that are set by the instructor. For example, annotations might summarise the main and supporting points of a text, assess the writer's position and credibility, and reflect how each text relates to the assignment.

2. Purpose of an Annotated Bibliography

Annotated bibliographies are used in academic and professional contexts, where the purpose of the annotation is to inform the reader of the relevance, accuracy, and quality of the sources listed. For example, The Educational Testing Services Network, which is responsible for the TOEFL (Test of English as a Foreign Language), offers a short bibliography of publications relevant to this test at its Web site (see http://www.ets.org/research/index.html). Each source is followed by a short annotation describing the main focus of the source. In addition, many university and college instructors give assignments that require students to compile an annotated bibliography. Such an assignment might be useful preparation for researching and writing on a selected topic, or it might allow you to demonstrate your familiarity with a topic.

Activity 2 | Sample Annotations

Look at the two sample annotations below. With a partner, discuss how they differ.

Sample 1

Biemiller, A. & Siegel, L.S. (1997). A longitudinal study of the effects of the Bridge reading program for children at risk for reading failure. *Learning Disability Quarterly*, 20 (2), 83-92.

This article reports on a longitudinal study designed to evaluate the Bridge program's effectiveness in improving learning disabled children's ability to read. The authors report significant improvements in study participants' ability to identify words.

Sample 2

Biemiller, A. & Siegel, L.S. (1997). A longitudinal study of the effects of the Bridge reading program for children at risk for reading failure. *Learning Disability Quarterly*, 20 (2), 83-92.

In this study, Biemiller and Siegel, internationally recognised researchers in reading, present data from a study of the importance of word identification for the development of reading. Their carefully constructed longitudinal study looked at a specific method of instruction, the Bridge program, and its effectiveness in leading to reading improvements in children with learning disabilities. The program uses a technique of matching icons with words until the word can be recognised visually without an accompanying icon. They concluded that the use of the Bridge program leads to significant improvement in students' ability to identify words. Biemiller and Siegel's work makes an important contribution to current insights into teaching methods that are appropriate for learning disabled children.

Activity 3 | Analysing an Evaluative Annotation

1. Read the annotation for a journal article in Sample 2 above.
2. Underline the author's point of view.
3. How does the author convey the authority of the source?
4. Does the author comment on the clarity and appropriateness of the source? Explain.

3. Types of Sources Used in an Annotated Bibliography

A broad range of sources may be used when compiling an annotated bibliography. A general guideline is that the source be available to others to consult. For example, published books would be suitable but lecture notes would not.

As a class

1. Brainstorm some of the various types of sources that you could use for a bibliography (e.g., government documents). The instructor or a volunteer should write down the sources suggested on the chalkboard or a similar display area.
2. Evaluate the sources, checking that each one is widely available.
3. Determine which sources would most likely be appropriate for academic and professional purposes.
4. Identify two or three sources that would not be suitable for inclusion in a bibliography.

4. Compiling an Annotated Bibliography

Four basic steps can be identified in the compilation of an annotated bibliography:

1. Before you can work on an annotated bibliography, you need to know its topic and consider its scope (the number and types of sources needed). Its scope will depend on the purpose of the annotated bibliography or the guidelines in a course assignment.
2. Locate the sources you need. This will likely require work in the library and may involve searches on the Internet.
3. Analyse the information in each of your sources. Make sure that you understand the information and take notes.
4. Write your citations and the annotations. Add a title and an introductory sentence or a paragraph.

Look at this section of an annotated bibliography.

Implications of Learning Disabilities for Developing Reading Abilities: Recent Research
Julie Paquette

Reading disabilities are frequently diagnosed in young children, yet little is known about how reading disabilities occur or how they can be overcome.

Johnson, L., Graham, S. & Harris, K. (1997). The effects of goal setting and self-instruction on learning a reading comprehension strategy: A study of students with learning disabilities. *Journal of Learning Disabilities*, 30 (1), 80-91.

This study looked at how efficient strategy instruction is in increasing the reading comprehension of children with learning disabilities. The authors defined learning disabilities as difficulties with different reading skills, such as word recognition, decoding, and comprehension. Specifically, they instructed student participants on how to use a story's grammar strategy. By doing so, the authors increased the reading comprehension of students with learning disabilities.

This article does not consider specific language impairments but demonstrates that when children with learning disabilities receive additional instruction, their reading comprehension can improve. In most cases, extra instruction allowed children to achieve the same reading level as their normal-reading peers.

Menyuk, P., Chesnick, M., Liebergott, J., Korngold, B., D'Agostino, R. & Belanger, A. (1991). Predicting reading problems in at-risk children. *Journal of Speech and Hearing Research*, 34, 893-903.

This study was conducted to determine which early language measures best predicted reading problems, especially in children with language disorders. Early measures of metalinguistic abilities or language awareness, rather than the degree of the child's delay, were found to be the best predictors of later reading problems.

The results from this study provide further evidence that language impairments do in fact affect children's reading ability. As well, the study states that metalinguistic abilities or amounts of language awareness have an impact on reading abilities.

Simmons, D., Fuchs, L., Fuchs, D., Mathes, P. & Hodge, J. (1995). Effects of explicit teaching and peer tutoring on the reading achievement of learning-disabled and low-performing students in regular classrooms. *The Elementary School Journal*, 95 (5), 387-408.

This study tried to discover whether students labelled as learning disabled benefit from explicit teaching and peer tutoring. Benefits were considered to occur if the students' reading achievement scores improved. The researchers found that the learning disabled students read more frequently after receiving both explicit teaching and peer tutoring. Their achievement scores increased significantly. However, reading scores did not improve significantly when students received only one of the two teaching treatments. The study gives some insight into the types of instructional methods that can help students overcome reading problems.

Activity 5   Analysing the Sample

1. What do you think were the intended purpose and audience? Explain your answer.
2. Why do the annotations not mention the authority of the source?
3. How could the annotations be improved?

Activity 6   Selecting a Topic

Prepare an annotated bibliography of four to six key sources on one of the following topics:
   a) Setting up a small business in your city
   b) Off-shore banking
   c) Selecting a university for graduate studies
   d) Evaluating Internet sources
   e) Healthy lifestyles
   f) The Nobel Prize

Activity 7   Preliminary Work

1. Work with two or three peers who have chosen the same topic. Discuss what the topic means to you.
2. Brainstorm possible purposes and audiences for your annotated bibliography.

3. Working individually, locate and analyse your sources.

4. Take notes in preparation for your annotations.

Activity 8   Taking on Each Source

The type of information included in an annotated bibliography and the level of detail included in each annotation depend on the intended purpose and audience.

1. On your own, make a list of the different types of information you might consider when taking notes for annotations.

2. Work with two or three partners once you have run out of ideas. Compare your lists.

3. Add to your list if necessary.

Annotations do not need a topic sentence, as the title of the item is understood as the topic. Brevity is important in annotations. Concentrate on meaning rather than on writing wordy sentences. Summarising skills are very important when writing annotations. Go back to Unit 6 if you need to review the basics about summary writing.

Activity 9   Writing the Annotations

Write annotations of 150-250 words for your annotated bibliography. Use full sentences. Each annotation should include

- a brief summary
- the authority of the source
- the author's (i.e., your) point of view, and
- how the source helps the intended audience.

Activity 10   Revising the Annotations

Working on your own,

1. Check that each annotation includes the information requested in Activity 8.

2. Make changes if necessary.

Working with the group you formed in Activity 7,

3. Read each other's annotations.

4. Ask questions if you do not understand parts of an annotation.

5. Offer comments, if appropriate, on how each peer might improve his or her annotations.

Working on your own,

6. Decide what suggestions to incorporate into your annotations. You may need to go back to your sources at this point to get more details or additional information.

Activity 11   Putting Together the Annotated Bibliography

1. Write the citations for your sources, following the APA format.

2. Give your annotated bibliography a descriptive title.

3. Write an introductory sentence to your annotated bibliography.

4. Add the revised annotations.

5. Check carefully that the citations contain all the required information. Check that the information follows the appropriate sequence.

6. Use your spell checker to verify the annotations.
7. Print out and hand in your annotated bibliography.

Summary of Real Life Writing Task 3

In this task you
- examined the differences between a list of references and a bibliography
- practised analysing and summarising longer texts
- wrote annotations, and
- compiled entries for an annotated bibliography.

REAL LIFE WRITING
THE ARGUMENTATIVE ESSAY

TASK 4

| Task 4 | REAL LIFE WRITING THE ARGUMENTATIVE ESSAY |

Objectives: - To write an argumentative essay
- To identify components of argumentation
- To practise giving support for one's own opinion and to anticipate the arguments that would be made against it
- To use connecting or transition words and phrases to show the relationship of two ideas

1. Purpose and Characteristics of Argumentative Essays

In an argumentative essay, the writer takes a stand on an issue and tries to persuade readers to agree with his or her opinion. An argument must focus on an idea that has two sides, one for and one against. In other words, an argument is debatable. One could not, for example, argue about a statement like

"A recent census shows that 86 percent of Argentina's population of 36,737,664 live in urban areas and 14 percent live in rural areas."

This is a statement of fact, verifiable in the relevant census, and does not have two opposing sides.

Whereas the main idea of a paragraph is a topic sentence, and the main idea of an essay is a thesis statement, the main idea in an argument is called a proposition. The proposition is the idea that writers want their readers to agree with. To provide a good argument, the proposition has to be stated clearly as one of the two sides of a topic.

| Activity 1 | **Raising Awareness** |

1. Look at the statements below. With a check mark (√), indicate which ones would be debatable.
2. Give your reasons for your judgements.
3. Reformulate those statements in question 1 that would not make good propositions. Turn them into good propositions. You may need to change or add to the information as several options are possible.

_____

_____

_____

_____

_____

_____

Statement	Debatable	
	yes	no
a) The government should enact laws to regulate cloning research.		
b) Women should serve in the military of their country.		
c) Drug smugglers caught in Singapore may face the death penalty.		
d) Changes need to be made in the law to find and punish cybercriminals.		
e) Solar energy is the best way of meeting the world's energy needs in the twenty-first century.		
f) A good education is essential for a successful and happy life.		
g) Computers and automation increase unemployment.		
h) Lack of exercise and poor eating habits lead to health problems.		
i) Governments are responsible for the prosperity of their citizens.		

Activity 2 **Write Your Own Statements**

1. Write a debatable and a non-debatable statement for each of the following topics.
   Alcohol   Transportation   Media   Copyright Laws

2. Compare your statements with those written by your peers.

2. Developing an Argument

As pointed out above, debatable statements are not statements of fact but are statements, or propositions, with which other people may agree or disagree. In an argumentative essay, the writer's purpose is to convince or persuade an audience to agree with the writer's point of view. To achieve this purpose, writers need to support their propositions through supporting statements. For example, a possible development for statement a) in Activity 1 above might be:

Topic: Cloning
Debatable statement: The government should enact laws to regulate cloning research.
Supporting statements:
   - Cloning leads to ethical problems, especially when the technique is applied to human cells.
   - Cloning is potentially harmful to human beings.

Both supporting statements lend support to the proposition, but the relationship between the proposition and its supporting arguments is not clearly stated. This relationship can be signalled with connecting words, also called *transition words* or *connectives*, as shown below (also see the Resource Centre, page 180):

The government should enact laws to regulate cloning research. *Firstly,* **cloning leads to ethical problems, especially when the technique is applied to human cells.** *In addition,* **cloning is potentially harmful to human beings.**

Connectives for Supporting Arguments	
Firstly	- signals the first supporting argument
Secondly	- signals the second supporting argument
Furthermore	- signals any additional or the final argument
Moreover In addition Finally	- signal the last supporting argument (but see below for the conclusion)
Connectives for Concluding Comments	
The conclusion should make final statements that address all your supporting arguments in a general way. It might start with one of the concluding connectives to signal to readers that you are bringing your argument to an end:	
In conclusion In summary	- signal final statements that cover all the supporting arguments in a general way; they convey roughly the same meaning

Activity 3 **Practise Supporting a Proposition**

1. Go back to the debatable statements you wrote in Activity 2. Add two or three supporting statements for each one.
2. Use connectives to link them to the propositions.
3. Compare your work with a partner's and discuss any differences you may have.

In an essay, the introduction contains the proposition (thesis statement). Each supporting statement is developed into a paragraph. More than one paragraph is required, as it will take more than one supporting argument to convince most readers of your point of view. The concluding paragraph should normally contain a repetition of the proposition. A visual representation of an argumentative essay might be:

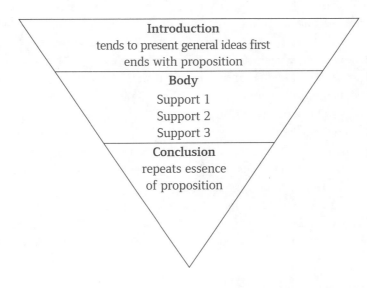

Introduction
tends to present general ideas first
ends with proposition

Body
Support 1
Support 2
Support 3

Conclusion
repeats essence
of proposition

3. Examining an Argumentative Essay

In preparation for writing an argumentative essay, examine a sample essay. Various activities will help you focus on important aspects in an argumentative essay.

Read the sample argumentative essay below. Be ready to answer questions.

Government Regulations for Cloning Research

Yin Mee Tang

The issue of whether governments should allow cloning research to proceed without restrictions has become an important question for scientists, politicians, ethicists, and religious leaders. The issue is important because it concerns fundamental moral and economic questions about the way scientific progress is made. A variety of different arguments have been put forward about this issue. This essay will consider arguments against government laws that regulate cloning research and point to some of the problems with these views. It will put forward reasons why governments should enact laws to regulate cloning research.

One of the main arguments that supporters of cloning research make is that cloning could result in significant benefits for human beings, including earlier diagnosis of certain diseases and better preventive medicines. Therapeutic cloning techniques, the argument goes, may lead to medicines, diagnostics, and vaccines to treat Alzheimer's Disease, Diabetes, Parkinson's, heart attacks, various cancers, and hundreds of other genetic diseases. Such advances have created considerable interest in human cloning, with some researchers indicating that they are working toward this very goal. However, other scientists point out the dangers of cloning humans and warn strongly against the dangers of cloning humans at this time. Moreover, Jaenisch and Wilmut (2001) call the current stage of research a "highly imperfect process" (p. 291) and suggest that any attempts at human cloning "...would be dangerous and irresponsible..."

Supporters of cloning research argue that the technology has been tested widely in animals and is ready to be tried in human beings. They point to Dolly, the successfully cloned sheep, to substantiate their argument. However, despite this success, Wilmut, Campbell, and Tudge (2000) point out that the efficiency of animal cloning in published work is very low. In fact, only around 2 percent of embryos created by cloning survive to term. The scientist who created Dolly made close to three hundred unsuccessful attempts at cloning a sheep before Dolly was born. Often, the embryos die during pregnancy, or soon after birth, and show developmental abnormalities, while their mothers miscarry and sometimes die too. Furthermore, many of those that do survive end up dying days or weeks later from kidney failure, cardiopulmonary failure, immune system deficiencies, or physical deformities (Wilmut, Campbell & Tudge, 2000). According to these researchers, it would be irresponsible to work on human cloning before the technique is further developed on various animals.

Another argument supporters of cloning research make is that it could help infertile parents have biological children. For example, it has been claimed that the technique could enable a couple who are both cystic fibrosis carriers to have their own child. Although few would consider such a procedure morally objectionable, some point to the dangers involved with the technique. As Cohen (1998) argues, the same techniques that may lead to positive results could also be abused. The same cloning technique could lead some to attempt to create a perfect child. Similarly, some people might want to clone an individual with special abilities, a dead child, or a special friend. If they were successful, the cloned individual might have a difficult life, trying to live up to the expectation that he or she will become as accomplished or do the same things as his or her genetic counterpart. This would surely be a morally objectionable use of the cloning technique.

In conclusion, cloning and genetic manipulation may offer benefits in the short run, but over time the consequences could be deadly. Several countries have temporarily banned human cloning, but in many others it is still legal. Governments need to work together to regulate cloning to ensure that new technologies are applied responsibly.

References

Cohen, P. (1998). Organs without Donors, *New Scientist*, Vol. 16, pp. 4-5.

Jaenisch, R. & Wilmut, I. (2001). Don't clone humans! *Science*, Vol. 291, No. 5513, p. 2552.

Kolata, G. (1997). *Clone the road to Dolly and beyond*. London: Penguin Press.

Wilmut, I., Campbell, K. & Tudge, C. (2000). *The second creation: The age of biological control by the scientists who cloned Dolly*. London: Headline Book Publishing.

Activity 5   Analyse the Example

Working as a class, discuss the two questions.
1. What is the argument the writer makes?
2. Is the essay convincing? Explain your answer.

Working on your own,
3. Underline the proposition or thesis in the essay. Write *P* in the margin next to the parts that express it.
4. Underline or highlight the supporting arguments. Write *A1, A2, A3* in the margin next to each.
5. Underline or highlight the conclusion, and then write *C* in the margin next to it.
6. Find the connecting words or phrases the author used. Circle them and identify their purpose.

Working with a partner,
7. Compare your answers and try to explain any differences.
8. Look at how the author supported each of the arguments made in the essay.

4. Writing an Argumentative Essay

Follow the remaining activities in this task and write an argumentative essay that will persuade an audience to accept your point of view.

Activity 6   Select a Topic

1. Unless your instructor assigns a specific topic, select one of the topics below.

Taxes	Free Trade	Modern Art	Immigration
Gambling	Genetic Testing	Cybercrime	Salaries for Athletes

2. Form groups with two or three peers who have selected the same topic.

Activity 7 — Explore the Issues

Work on your own for the first three items, and then work with the group you formed in Activity 6.
1. Think about what the topic you selected means to you, and then write down your ideas.
2. Give an example that illustrates your meaning.
3. Think about attitudes and opinions that members of society might have toward your topic. Write down your ideas in point format.
4. Discuss your ideas with your group members. Take additional notes if necessary.

You will likely need to do some research in the library or on the Internet to add more detail to the ideas in your notes.

The seven steps below will help you organise your notes and develop a first draft. You may need to go back to your sources or do some additional research to help you develop your ideas.

Activity 8 — Develop a First Draft

1. Determine your proposition and write a statement that expresses your point of view.
2. Use the notes to form groups of similar ideas suitable for main arguments.
3. Identify the two to four strongest main arguments.
4. Formulate a sentence that will serve as a topic sentence for each main argument. Each of these sentences will provide the topic sentence of a paragraph.
5. From your notes, find supporting arguments for each main argument.
6. Develop them into sentences and paragraphs.
7. Write an introductory and a concluding paragraph.

Activity 9 — Revising and Editing

1. Read your draft carefully. Check for the following and make changes where appropriate:
   a) Is there a clear point of view expressed in your proposition?
   b) Are your main arguments presented the way you want them?
   c) Is each main argument supported?
   d) Are the different ideas linked to show how they are related to each other?
   e) Are you convinced by your own arguments?
2. Write down any problems you feel remain in your draft. List questions you would like to discuss with a reader.
3. Ask a partner to review the specific problems and questions you noted in 2 and take note of the feedback you receive.
4. Think about your partner's feedback and decide how you can use it to improve your draft.
5. Use the Editing Checklist to edit your draft for grammar and mechanical problems.
6. Write a second draft of your argumentative essay.

Activity 10   Publishing

1. Meet with the members of the group you formed in Activity 7 and read each other's essays.
2. Collect the essays and display them on the class bulletin board for all class members to read.
3. Identify the most convincing essay on each topic and submit it for publication ("Letters from Readers" in your school or local paper; alternately, your teacher might be able to arrange for them to be published on your class or school's Web site).

Summary of Real Life Writing Task 4

In this task you
- examined the characteristics of an argument
- studied the features of an argumentative essay
- developed ideas for an argumentative essay
- wrote and published your essay.

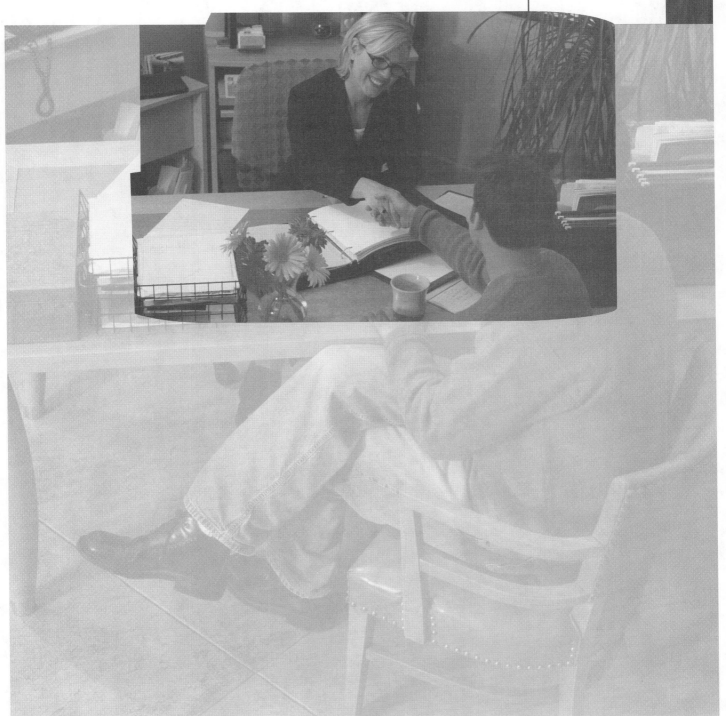

REAL LIFE WRITING
WRITING A RESUME AND COVER LETTER

Objectives: - To analyse the contents of a resume
- To develop a resume
- To write a cover letter

The focus of this task is to reflect on past education and experience, to gather information, to list information related to these areas, and to use it to put together a two-page resume and cover letter that could be used to apply for a desired position.

1. Background Information: The Resume

A resume is an outline of an individual's education, professional history, and experience, summarised in no more than two pages. Its organisation typically follows either a chronological or a functional organisation. A chronological resume gives the information about education and work experience in chronological (time) sequence, starting with the most recent and ending with the least recent information. Skills and achievements are added below each of the chronological items. A chronological resume is easy for a potential employer to read and assess quickly. However, if an individual has been out of the workforce for some time or has had to change jobs a number of times, which may be seen as a disadvantage, this will be quickly obvious.

A functional resume focuses on an individual's skills and accomplishments as related to the job for which he or she is applying. This format may be helpful for those who are just joining or have been out of the workforce for some time, or for individuals who have been involved in regular volunteer work. A functional resume presents an individual's strengths and avoids a focus on his or her work history. Some employers, however, have misgivings about the absence of chronological details in a functional resume.

A combination of chronological and functional organisation may be useful for some job seekers. Whatever its format, a resume should reflect logical organisation, clear layout, and action verbs that highlight an individual's skills and accomplishments. In addition, a resume should be updated regularly to reflect an individual's new skills and experience. Recent publications of resume guides in libraries, student centres, or on the Internet may contain examples for specific professions or job categories.

Purpose of a resume:
- to show a potential employer your education and experience
- to highlight your skills and abilities, especially those related to the position applied for
- to make these easily accessible to a reader, the potential employer (employers typically take about three minutes to skim and scan a resume to decide whether they have any interest in the applicant).

Content of a resume:
- is geared toward the position applied for
- includes relevant information about work and volunteer experience
- presents an overview of educational achievements and special courses related to work
- relates presentations given at conferences
- notes publications written or co-written by the individual
- is accurate in all respects
- contains sufficient information that can be verified by the receiver.

A resume may include an objective statement or statement of career goals. This statement is expressed in a short sentence or sentence fragment. It may indicate what
- **position the applicant is applying/looking for**
- **career goals the applicant has**
- **key qualifications the applicant offers.**

Many resumes do not include such a statement as applicants may feel it will limit their options with a given employer.

Format of a resume:
- generally has either a functional or a chronological focus
- commonly has no more than two pages
- uses bullets to draw attention to important information
- says that references are usually provided on request (but references could alternately be included on a third page)
- requires neatness, correctness, and attractiveness if the writer is to make a good impression.

Specific information offered and its sequence in a resume:
Applicant's
- name
- contact information
- statement of objective (if offered)
- educational background
- experience
- honours, relevant activities

2. Getting Started

Activity 1 | **Awareness Raising**

Read through the following two resumes and answer the questions that follow. Then share your answers with a small group.
1. Which resume uses a chronological format? Which is functional?
2. What has the writer done to make it easy for the reader to identify his or her skills and abilities quickly?
3. What language is used to help the reader think that the writer is a hard-working and skilled candidate for a job?

Example 1

Lee Catalan
357 Frances Avenue, Toronto, Ontario, M2G 6K7
(416) 685-3869

EDUCATION

Master of Education in TESL (1996)
Terrant University, Lakeview, Ontario, L2R 3B7
A average

Bachelor of Education (1991)
Terrant University, Lakeview, Ontario, L2R 3B7
A average

Bachelor of Arts (1989)
Coyne University, Gordon, Pennsylvania 20670
A average; Major: Psychology

EMPLOYMENT
Co-ordinator, Writing Skills

Department of English Language & Linguistics, Terrant University
September 1992 - present

- lead workshops for new teachers
- maintain files
- develop materials
- observe and assist classroom teachers
- write reports
- monitor lesson plans
- mentor teacher

ESL Teacher

Department of English Language & Linguistics, Terrant University
July 1991 - present

- teach Reading, Writing, Grammar, Speaking, and Lab Skill areas
- prepare lessons, assignments, activities, and exams
- evaluate students' work
- assist with placement testing
- participate in outings and activities with students

Professional Associations: TESL Ontario, TESOL

Presented workshops:

TESL Ontario 1993 – Authentic Writing Tasks

TESL Ontario 1994 – Student Participation in Course Development

TESL Canada 1997 – Writing on the Web

TESL Ontario 1999 – Collocations in the Writing Class

Publications:

Write in Person (1998, Alwright Publishers), co-author of this beginning-level writing text

OTHER EMPLOYMENT

Happy Days Restaurant

Lakeview, Ontario

September 1989–May 1990

- supervised and trained new employees
- co-ordinated and planned special events

Career Assistant

Counselling Centre, Terrant University

July 1990–April 1991

- assisted students in the career planning process
- critiqued resumes
- assisted in the hiring process
- planned and implemented projects as part of a team

Teaching Assistant

Research Assistant

Psychology Department, Terrant University

Professor James Doherty

September 1987–May 1990

- facilitated group discussion in seminars
- marked examinations
- ran subjects for a study

Other Relevant Experience

- assisted and led courses in parent education
- developed and implemented a bimonthly luncheon and programme for senior citizens
- acted as chairperson of the Diocesan Christian Education Committee. Chaired meetings, prepared budgets, designed and implemented teacher training programmes.
- Conference Work: co-ordinated a team to prepare and present small conferences. Made presentations, organised training sessions, arranged timetables, facilitated the group process.

References available on request.

Example 2

Mary Ellen Penfield

12 Catharine Street

Windfall, Alaska, 99599

USA

Education

1993 – 1997 Bachelor of Journalism

Ryerson Polytechnic Institute, Toronto

Relevant courses include:

- Public Relations Theory and Practice
- Media Ethics and the Law
- Information Resources
- Copy Editing
- Broadcast Reporting
- Page Layout and Design
- Journalism and Photography
- Print Reporting

Skills and Abilities

Communication:

- produced clear broadcast copy (University Newscast)
- generated media coverage and advertising using phone skills
- created and delivered lectures using PowerPoint and other technical programmes

Interpersonal:

- worked well in group environments expediting national campaign to raise money for The Association for Children with Learning Disabilities
- managed a maintenance crew of thirteen summer staff in a city park

Technical:

- employed videotape equipment to produce news features
- excellent competency with WP, MS Word, PowerPoint, Corel Draw
- used skills in layout and design to produce class magazine and leaflets

Time Management:

- consistently met all deadlines for publication
- organised the assignments and scheduling of 25 members of News Staff
- administered budget and payment of expenses for parks staff
- selected by management as Employee of the Month for assistance in work overload

   - managed the scheduling of steps in production of advertising leaflet for the Centre for Learning Disabilities

Additional Information:

- won the Governor General's Prize for High School Journalism
- published articles in the local press on entertainment and local history
- achieved awards for photography in the Atlantic and Central Regional Photographic Competitions
- free to relocate and to travel on the job
- speak fluent Japanese and Spanish, some French
- completed a certificate in small business accounting practices
- own a reliable vehicle

References and Portfolio available on request

As you develop your resume, it is important to gather all the information you will need. For a chronological resume fill in the information below.

1. Education

   List your educational certificates, diplomas, or degrees, the year you completed each one, and the name of the school and the city in which the school is located. You may also add grades, awards, and honours.

Degree/Diploma	Year	School/University	City
_____	_____	_____	_____
_____	_____	_____	_____
_____	_____	_____	_____
_____	_____	_____	_____

2. Work Experience

   Make a list of your full-time and part-time jobs, including summer and volunteer work as well as any field placement or work experiences. List them in chronological order, starting from the most recent.

   You need to include information about the job title, the employer's name, the location, and the dates in which you were employed. List skills used, responsibilities, and any specific accomplishments. Focus on your duties and accomplishments by listing action words (see the lists that follow for vocabulary suggestions). Keep in mind the job you are applying for and those skills and tasks that would be most applicable.

Job	Dates	Employer	Location	Skills Used
_____	_____	_____	_____	_____
_____	_____	_____	_____	_____
_____	_____	_____	_____	_____
_____	_____	_____	_____	_____

3. Extracurricular Activities

   Make a list of your memberships in clubs, professional associations you belong to, community and volunteer experiences, hobbies, interests, sports, and any elected positions you have held. List beside them any skills practised or learned and any personal qualities exhibited or developed.

Activity	Skills Used	Personal Qualities
_____	_____	_____
_____	_____	_____
_____	_____	_____
_____	_____	_____

4. References

Make a list of people willing to give you a reference. You should have their names, positions, addresses, and telephone numbers. It is best if you choose people who can discuss your abilities and accomplishments in the following areas: employment (previous employer), academic (professor or teaching assistant), and personal (friend or co-worker). Having more than one possibility on your list means that you can select references best suited to a particular job application.

Possible References (Give Full Names)

Employer Reference	Position	Address	Telephone
_____	_____	_____	_____
_____	_____	_____	_____
_____	_____	_____	_____

Academic Reference	Position	Address	Telephone
_____	_____	_____	_____
_____	_____	_____	_____
_____	_____	_____	_____

Personal Reference	Position	Address	Telephone
_____	_____	_____	_____
_____	_____	_____	_____
_____	_____	_____	_____

5. Read through the following list. If the quality is one you possess, write an example of a situation in which you displayed the quality. This information will be useful in the resume, cover letter, and interview situation. The more aware you are of your own qualities and abilities, the more able you will be to sell yourself to a future employer. Do this in your notebook by listing ideas under these headings:

Personal Quality/Skill

Examples When Used

_____   _____

_____   _____

_____   _____

_____   _____

Some Personal Qualities:

accepting of feedback	analytical	articulate	assertive
calm under pressure	cheerful	conscientious	cooperative
courteous	creative	reliable	flexible
honest	industrious	leadership ability	motivated
organised	persuasive	punctual	resourceful
self-directed	time management		

Some Skills Used:

administration	auditing	budgeting	coaching
diagnosing/assessing	editing	facilitating	handling complaints
interviewing	managing	meeting deadlines	organising
planning/preparing	promoting	speaking	recording
researching	selling	supervising	teaching/training

Activity 3 **Writing Your Resume**

1. Decide which format you will use: chronological or functional.
2. Think about layout. You can find examples in resume books from the library or a bookstore, or you can use a layout similar to the two examples in this unit.
3. Remember to use a heading with your name, address, and phone number.
4. Type the resume, making it as attractive as possible, and using bullets to highlight skills.
5. Print your resume to check that its appearance is neat and attractive. Read it over carefully, checking for typing errors, spelling errors, or any inaccuracies.

Activity 4 **Peer Review**

In small groups, review each resume.
1. Read them through for accuracy.
2. Discuss any possible changes that might make them more attractive.

3. The Cover Letter

To write a good cover letter, you need to understand its purpose and usual content.

Purpose:

- to give the author's reason for writing
- to show the author's suitability for the job
- to indicate why the author wants to work for the company in question
- to ask for an interview and suggest a convenient time

Content:

Both the cover letter and the resume should respond to a careful reading of the advertisement for the position. They should contain

- a reference to the position applied for and information about how the resume writer heard of it
- highlights that show the candidate's suitability for the position (and a reference to an attached resume, which contains more complete information)
- an indication that the potential employee has knowledge and interest in the company

Format:

The format of a cover letter is the same as that of any formal business letter.

Activity 5 **Looking at an Example**

Read the following cover letter. Be prepared to discuss it with your class or in a group.

Example Cover Letter:

Lee Catalan
357 Frances Avenue
Toronto, Ontario, M2G 6K7

May 31, 2002

Janice E. Smith
Director
Toronto English Schools Inc.
666 Yonge Street
Toronto, Ontario, M5W 3S6

Dear Ms Smith:

I am writing in response to your advertisement in the *Toronto Star* of May 29 for an Assistant Director in charge of curriculum development and testing for your schools in the Ontario area. Working for your schools would provide me with experience in the private sector at an ESL school of the highest quality. Your focus on the use of practical, communicative tasks in the classroom, and the continued research and development of your program put your schools in the forefront of the private sector of ESL teaching. The position of Assistant Director in charge of curriculum development and testing would also allow me to further my career in both curriculum development and administration.

As you can see from my enclosed resume, I have considerable experience in testing, teaching, curriculum and materials development, as well as in supervision and training. You will find my enthusiasm and experience to be advantageous to the development of your schools in Ontario.

I have recently moved to the Toronto area for the summer and would be available for an interview at your convenience. I would welcome an opportunity to discuss my eligibility for the position and the ways in which my past experience and present interests make me an ideal candidate. You can reach me at 416-123-3869.

I am looking forward to hearing from you.

Yours sincerely,

Lee Catalan

Lee Catalan

encl 1

Activity 6 — Information in the Cover Letter

Discuss the following questions.
1. What job is the author applying for?
2. What does the author say that shows this position fits his or her experience?
3. How does he or she show that the position/company is attractive to him or her?
4. What are the topics of each paragraph in the letter?
5. What word shows that the resume has been mailed with the letter?
6. What does *encl 1* mean? Why is it there?

Activity 7 — Writing a Cover Letter

Find a newspaper or Internet advertisement for a job that you would like. The job should suit your skills. Underline the qualifications and skills the advertisement is asking for.
Write a cover letter to request an interview for the job.
Paragraph 1: Indicate why you are writing and where you heard about the job.
Paragraph 2: Discuss why this position and this company are attractive to you.
Paragraph 3: Show briefly why hiring you would benefit the company.
Paragraph 4: Request an interview and tell them how to get in touch with you.

Activity 8 — Peer Review

Exchange letters with a partner and discuss these questions.
1. Is the format of the letter correct?
2. Is the content clear and straightforward?
3. Has the author included all the necessary information?

4. Does the letter indicate that it is accompanied by a resume?

5. Does the author ask for an interview and suggest a way to contact him or her?

Summary of Real Life Task 5

In this task you
- analysed two resumes and a cover letter
- developed your resume
- wrote a cover letter.

Additional Activities

1. List questions that might be asked at the interview you requested in your letters. If necessary, borrow a job-hunting book or search the Internet for potential questions.

2. Form groups of three. Two people take the role of the employers and one the applicant. This will give you practice talking about the things you can do and about your experiences. Change roles so everyone gets a chance to be the candidate for the job.

REAL LIFE WRITING
WRITING A BUSINESS REPORT

Task 6

REAL LIFE WRITING
WRITING A BUSINESS REPORT

Objectives: - To write a short business report as a member of a team
- To practise the use of the rhetorical pattern of comparison and contrast
- To use appropriate transition words
- To incorporate information from a consumer taste test

The purpose of this task is to illustrate the conventions of writing a short business report. Part of this particular report involves incorporating information gathered from a consumer taste test. The report provides practice in applying the rhetorical pattern of comparison and contrast. Finally, the task gives you practice in preparing the report as a team.

1. General Explanations

Writing business reports is a common real life activity. A business report is a formal writing assignment with a multi-paragraph structure in which the contents of the sections are clearly defined. Report writing of any kind should be straightforward and concise. The ideas should be stated clearly and briefly. Flowery words and long sentences do not belong in business reports. The format of a report is designed to make the content easily accessible to the reader through the use of section headings.

Business reports vary in length and type. The one included in this unit is for a short business case. It is common both in the business world and in academic business courses to work on such reports in groups. For this reason, and also to reduce the length of this assignment, this will be a group assignment. Common mistakes that result in ineffective reports and possibly loss of marks include the following: poor presentation (not typed, not double-spaced, grammar problems, spelling errors, typographical errors), carelessness, lack of clarity, illogical arguments, and lack of analysis.

2. Guidelines on the Business Report Format

The business report should have a title page. Instructors usually require that the instructor's name, the student's name and identification number, and the due date be printed in the lower right-hand side (similar to the cover page for a research paper; see Cover Page in the Resource Centre, page 177).

A business report should be divided into sections with appropriate headings. In a longer report, a table of contents, listing the sections and their page numbers, is important as it makes the material more accessible to the reader. The basic sections required in many reports, including the one in this unit, are these:

a) Introduction

An introduction consists of one clear and concise paragraph giving relevant background information. It identifies the key question that must be resolved and looks at any issues or problems arising from the key problem.

b) Situation Analysis

This section identifies alternatives that may solve the problem. Alternatives are mutually exclusive. Group members use the group's decision criteria, and incorporate any relevant material from the case. They use logical skills and common sense. Statements need to be substantiated with evidence. Any calculations and lengthy explanations are placed into appendices.

c) Recommendation

This section should consist of one paragraph that identifies the best alternative, the one with the least risk. The alternative should solve the problem with the resources available.

d) Implementation

This section can be written in point form or as two or three paragraphs. It should identify operational plans, short-term and long-term plans, resources needed, and the expected results.

e) Appendices

This section should include relevant financial statements, graphs, extensive explanations, and calculations.

3. A Business Case

The next page presents the layout of a sample business report. A number of activities follow the presentation of the business report.

CMV Canada: Steering Wheel Function Report

Submitted by: The Chelsea Group

Student ID Number: 132567
Instructor: [add name]
For: CMV Corporation
Due: July 1, 2002

Introduction

This report is in response to your request of January 1999. The advertising department of CMV were concerned with the number of complaints received about the new style of steering wheel. Apparently, several letters of complaint regarding the wheel had been received and a decision about whether to continue its use must be made. Our firm was asked to implement a market survey and make a recommendation as to whether or not this new model of steering wheel should be dropped.

Situation Analysis

Our firm identified three alternatives. First, use of the new steering wheel could be continued at present. Second, the new steering wheel could be continued with minor alterations that would address customer concerns and complaints. Third, the new steering wheel could be discontinued and the former model could be reinstated. In order to make a recommendation, we conducted customer trials with both the old and the new steering wheels. We interviewed the customers, using a questionnaire to assess the level of satisfaction with each steering wheel. Three criteria were used as a basis of comparison: handling, control in difficult situations, and comfort. In our view, if the majority of customers were satisfied with these points, the steering wheel could be continued as is. This information would also inform us about any modifications that might improve the levels of customer satisfaction.

Survey Results and Recommendations

Results of our customer survey indicated that customers were satisfied with the handling and control of the steering mechanism. With regard to the handling of the steering wheels, they felt that the new model handled as well as the previous model. Most customers thought that the new model handled as well as the

-1-

previous model. Most customers thought that the new model handled even better on sharp turns than the old one, and they had a greater sense of control in using it. On the other hand, many of those in the trial complained that the steering wheel was more slippery than the old model and, at times, they thought they might lose control. The second criteria we assessed was control in different situations. To test this, customers were asked to run through a number of gates and turns at reasonably high speeds, with quick stops at flag points. There was unanimous agreement among participants that the new steering wheel performed much better under these conditions than the older model did. Once again, some participants complained of the texture of the plastic, finding it more slippery than the older model, and a slight cause for concern. Finally, customers were questioned about the comfort of the wheel in use. Although five mentioned the slippery feel of the wheel, 18 out of 20 of the participants said that the overall size and shape of the new wheel were more comfortable than the one used in the past. In every way, customers seemed most satisfied with the new model of steering wheel, rather than the previous model. However, there were consistent complaints concerning the slippery feel of the new wheel, which we think would be important to address.

In light of these findings, we recommend that the new wheel be continued because customers show a significantly higher degree of satisfaction with the new model. However, we also recommend that minor alterations be made to the texture of the plastic to increase the customers' sense that they have a solid grip. This alteration should not increase costs greatly and would solve the problem that we suspect was the basis of the initial complaints that resulted in your request for a survey of customer reaction. This small modification would, in our view, increase the level of customer satisfaction overall.

-2-

As a homework assignment,
    1. Read the explanations and the sample business report.
    2. Underline the most important ideas.

Activity 2   **Awareness Raising**

In small groups, develop an outline in point format that lists the main points in each section of the report. Refer to the underlined sections in your homework. Write your outline on a separate sheet of paper using Roman numerals for each section of the report and letters for each main point within a section, as shown below. Adjust the outline example to suit your report. A more detailed discussion of the numbering system used in outlines can be found in Task 7, pages 162-163.

    I. Introduction
        A.
        B.
        C.
    II. Situation Analysis

    III. Survey Results and Recommendations

Analyse the construction of the sample business report carefully and use the above outline as a model for the construction of a similar report in a later section of this unit. Some more detailed analysis in the following will help reinforce the basic concepts.

Activity 3   **Questions**

In small groups, answer the following questions in the space provided. Keep notes on a separate sheet of paper.

    1. What questions are answered by the information in each section?

_____

_____

    2. What characteristics identify this as formal writing?

_____

_____

3. How does the example differ from other writing you have done?

_____

_____

4. Who is the intended audience of this business report?

_____

_____

5. What purpose does the business report serve?

_____

_____

4. Writing the Report

You are part of a marketing team for Canada National Grocers, a firm that distributes groceries to independent grocery stores. Your marketing team has been asked to do a market survey of consumers' preferences for one of two types of chocolate chip cookies. You have been asked to write a brief report recommending that one of the two be distributed to grocery stores served by Canada National Grocers.

Materials: Two different types of chocolate chip cookies in sufficient quantities to supply at least one of each type to each student. The cookies should be wrapped in paper, marked for either Type A or Type B. The markings should not be visible. Putting the cookies onto two types of napkins helps keep Types A and B easily distinguishable.

Activity 4   Gathering Information

As a class,

1. Brainstorm categories that could be used to compare the cookies. Choose appropriate adjectives that could be used for each category.
   Example: *category*: texture   *adjective*: rough

_____

_____

_____

_____

2. Using the cookie comparison chart below, taste-test the cookies and fill in the form.

Chocolate Chip Cookie Comparison Chart		
Characteristic	**Cookie Type A**	**Cookie Type B**
Price		
Number of cookies per bag		
Number of calories per cookie		
Amount of fat per cookie		
Amount of chocolate		
Texture a) b) c)		
Appearance a) b) c)		
Taste a) b) c)		

Activity 5   Form Business Groups

1. Divide the class into groups of four. Each group represents a marketing team.
2. Discuss each of the categories and decide which type of cookie the members of your group prefer. Although they may not prefer one type of cookie in each category, they should identify an overall choice. For example, if cookie A is preferred for taste, but cookie B is preferred for price, the group should identify either cookie A or cookie B as an overall choice.
3. Develop an outline for the relevant sections of the business report, recommending your group's choice.

Activity 6   Writing the Draft Report

Select one of these methods for your draft report:

a) Write the report as a group, delegating one section to each group member. Each group member writes the rough draft of the section for which he or she is responsible. Then, the group goes through the peer feedback procedure in Activity 7.

or

b) Each group member drafts a report based on the findings of the team. They exchange reports in preparation for Activity 7.

Activity 7   Peer Feedback and Revision

Consider the draft reports in view of the following questions:

1. Does each section contain all the necessary information?
2. Are the supporting ideas in logical order?
3. Is the writing formal, clear, and concise?
4. Are the conclusions drawn logical? Can they be supported?
5. Is the format attractive and neat? Are appropriate headings for sections used?
6. Does the report fulfill its purpose?

Revise the report according to the feedback received.

Activity 8   Editing

Edit the revised version of the report. Use the following to guide you:

1. Check spelling.
2. Are transition words used appropriately?
3. Is there agreement between subjects and verbs in each sentence?
4. Read your draft carefully to check for errors in punctuation, spelling, and grammar.
5. Make final changes and corrections, and then produce the final draft to hand in for evaluation.

Remember that business writing is formal, clear, and concise. An attractive, professional appearance is very important in business writing. This includes creating a suitable cover page and, for longer reports, a table of contents and appendices containing financial information or graphs. Business reports can range in length from little more than a memo to over a hundred pages. Check with your instructor for details if a table of contents and appendices are required.

Summary of Real Life Writing Task 6

In this task you
- studied the components of a business report
- worked in small groups to simulate a marketing team
- drafted, reviewed, and revised a short business report based on the findings of your group
- practised the use of transitions in multi-paragraph writing.

Alternate Activities and Additional Topics

1. Brainstorm ideas on other products you might want to taste-test (e.g., coffee, soft drinks, tea), either within your class or your institution. Arrange the testing and then write the report.

2. In small groups, think of an organisation or institution and the type of consumer information it might like to have. For example, a department store trying to work out its opening hours might want to know when consumers prefer to do their shopping; a CD distributor might want to know how and where people prefer to buy their CDs; a restaurant might want to know what additional or alternate items its clients might like to see on the menu; a group of investors might want to find out whether there is a market for their franchise (e.g., sports equipment, brand name clothes) on campus. Identify a topic, and then arrange a relevant survey of a small group of consumers. Write the report. Display the final reports in your class or institution.

REAL LIFE WRITING
THE RESEARCH PAPER

TASK 7

| Task 7 | REAL LIFE WRITING THE RESEARCH PAPER |

Objectives: - To research ideas for a research paper
- To write a research paper
- To incorporate ideas from two or three sources
- To use notecards to organise your ideas and sources
- To apply skills practised in earlier units

The focus of this task is on integrating a number of different aspects of the writing process into one larger piece of formal writing, which will be a research paper on the general topic of *lies*. Before launching into the main topic, you should think about what the term *research paper* means to you.

1. Getting Started

Activity 1   Awareness Raising

1. On a piece of paper, write down in point format what the expression *research paper* means to you.
2. Do not make judgements about your ideas, for there is no "right" or "wrong" meaning. Just write your ideas as they occur to you.
3. When you have written down all your ideas, compare your list with that of a partner and make any changes you consider necessary.
4. Report two or three of your ideas to the whole class. Listen carefully to hear your peers' ideas.
5. Discuss some similarities between your ideas and those of your peers.

Next, you will read a short research paper. As you read the paper, you will be asked to think about specific questions that are particularly important for more formal writing.

Activity 2   Review

As you read the research paper "Culture Shock: Stages and Rages," answer the following questions:
1. What is the purpose of the paper?

_____

2. Who is its likely audience?

_____

3. What is its thesis?

_____

4. What is the main idea/topic sentence of each paragraph?

_____

_____

_____

_____

5. Look carefully at the paper, then fill in the *Outline* of main ideas below.

OUTLINE: Introduction _____

Second paragraph: _____

Third paragraph: _____

Fourth paragraph: _____

Fifth paragraph: _____

Conclusions: _____

6. What do you notice about the size and development of paragraphs?

_____

_____

_____

_____

7. In small groups, compare your answers and decide which ones are most appropriate. If necessary, combine the answers of several group members.

Culture Shock: Stages and Rages

   Hiro had always thought of himself as a good student, a reasonable, responsible, and reliable young man. But he found it difficult to understand what was happening to him now. One day his friend asked him a question and he snapped back with an angry response. His study habits had gone "down the tubes," as his Canadian friends would say. He felt depressed and angry much of the time. Everything his host family said and did seemed unreasonable. He hated the sound of English and the way Canadians behaved. What could be wrong with him, he wondered. It is possible he was suffering from culture shock. Understanding culture shock and its causes is important for people living in a foreign country. If they are aware of the symptoms and how to deal with them, their stay can be more fulfilling.

Culture shock is a condition that is commonly experienced by people who are living in a second culture. According to Brown (1980:81) it refers to "a phenomenon ranging from mild irritability to deep psychological panic and crisis." This implies that there can be great variations in the degree to which culture shock affects people. We could compare it to the common cold. A cold can last for two days to two weeks. Occasionally a cold can escalate into something more serious like pneumonia or bronchitis. The individual's health, habits, ability to recognise and react to the symptoms, and the atmosphere surrounding the person are all factors that affect the seriousness of a cold. A multitude of factors may also be related to the degree of seriousness of culture shock. Being aware of the condition and the symptoms is an important first step in dealing with the problem.

The symptoms of culture shock are many and varied. Brown (1980) notes that some of the feelings associated with culture shock are anger, sadness, loneliness, homesickness, and even physical illness. The person may alternate between feelings of anger and self-pity, according to Brown. Oberg (1993:31) identifies more detailed symptoms such as "excessive washing of hands, excessive concern over drinking water, food dishes, and bedding ...an absentminded stare, a feeling of helplessness" or "great concern over minor pains and eruptions of the skin." These symptoms may all be coupled with a dreadful desire to be back home.

Both authorities agree that there appear to be stages in the successful adjustment to a new culture, and culture shock may be one of them. These include a first stage of excitement after arrival. Everything is interesting and new. People are kind and thoughtful and dote on the new visitor. If the person stays for a longer period of time, this euphoria is unlikely to last when he or she has to deal with real situations or difficulties. Obvious symptoms of culture shock may begin here. At this time, a new stage begins when the visitor becomes aggressive and even hostile to the host country. Even when native speakers help, they do not seem to understand the difficulties. At this stage, the visitors often band together with those from their own country. They may be highly critical of the host country and stereotype the people. If visitors do not work through this stage to new understandings, they may leave and go home. Next, the visitors may take a stoic attitude that says "This is my problem and I have to bear it." They may develop a sense of superiority to the people of the host country, and a sense of humour about their own difficulties. By the final stage, the visitors make a complete adjustment, accept the new country, and operate there without anxiety, although there may be moments of difficulty and strain.

There is no easy cure for culture shock. As with most problems, understanding that it is a common problem for all who live in a different culture takes some of the strain of self-doubt away. Preparation for such a venture may make it less difficult. Part of the problem is the strangeness of the new culture, so the more one can understand what one is getting into, the less stressful the adjustment will be. Social networks have long been understood to help people through crisis, so the development of a number of friendships with individuals who are understanding and helpful may be another way to resist serious problems with culture shock. Maintaining a healthy lifestyle with exercise, rest, and good food also helps one to cope with stress, a very real result of living in a foreign environment. Remembering that there is light at the end of the tunnel–that many people have worked their way through this series of stages to an acceptance of the new culture and an ability to function in it–is in itself an encouragement in times of difficulty.

Hiro, with whom the essay started, was one of these people. After a period of difficulty, he adjusted well to his new environment. Now a successful international businessman, he can operate in two languages and two cultures. He is a more interesting and more understanding person as a result of his experience. He successfully worked through his "culture shock." You can too.

References

Brown, H.D. (1980). *Principles of language learning*. Englewood Cliffs, NJ: Prentice-Hall.

Oberg, K. (1993) Culture shock and the problem of adjustment in new cultural environments. In E.M. Baudoin, E. Buber, M. Clarke, B. Dobson & S. Silberstein (Eds.), *Reader's Choice*, 30-33. Ann Arbor, MI: University of Michigan Press.

2. Gathering Ideas

Now that you have reviewed the organisation and content of a sample paper, you are ready to gather ideas for your own paper.

| Activity 3 | **Exploring the Topic "Lies"** |

The general topic for your research paper is "Lies." The questions below will help you think about the topic, but you might want to check the library or the Internet for additional ideas.

1. Write your definitions and answers to the following questions:

A) What are lies?

_____

_____

B) Do you think there are different kinds of lies? For example "good" and "bad" lies? Explain.

_____

_____

C) When and where have you encountered lies?

_____

_____

D) What might make you tell a lie?

_____

_____

2. Compare your responses to the above questions with those of a partner. What similarities and differences are there between the two sets of answers?

| Activity 4 | **Brainstorming Different Academic Fields of Study** |

Before you narrow down your topic, it is important to explore the possibilities. That way you are more likely to find a focused topic and research questions that will really interest you.

1. As a class activity, list across the board the majors that people choose in their university studies.
2. Under each major, list how lies might be of interest in that subject area. For example:

BUSINESS

- why business people might lie
- difference between lying and withholding information
- difference between making a statement that represents a lie and a statement that is misleading (e.g., in advertising)

CHILD STUDIES

- reasons children lie
- teaching children to be truthful
- recognising children's lies

| Activity 5 | **A Different Perspective** |

Read the text below by Giselle Reike. As you read it, underline the definitions of lies and the ways in which a person can tell if another person is telling a lie.

Detecting Lies
Giselle Reike

Have you ever wondered if someone was telling the truth? Likely you have, as most people do from time to time. When I was a child, my mother used to say "Look in my eyes" when she suspected I was telling a lie. Often she seemed to know. I thought she could read my mind or that there was something in my eyes that gave away the fact that I really had broken the vase or eaten the forbidden candy. It is important before going farther that we define what is meant by the word *lie*. Ekman (1997) states that a lie is more than mere falsification. In his view, a lie is distinguished by the fact that the liar deliberately chooses to mislead the target; the liar does not notify the target about the intention to mislead. For Ekman, concealing truths by using half truths, incorrect inferences, and telling the truth in such a way as to lead a person to think one means the opposite are as much lies as falsification. Research seems to have found some ways that can be used to recognise lies, but it is difficult for most of us to do so with accuracy.

Verbal clues are the first ways that can be used to identify a lie. According to Ekman (1997), lies may be obvious when the liar is asked a question he or she is not prepared for or when the person has forgotten a previous lie and contradicts himself or herself. In this case, the telltale sign is the information given verbally. Ekman goes on to say that when someone is lying, such verbal clues as pauses, a lack of fluency in the speech, and some speech mannerisms may all occur more frequently than is usual for the person. He also notes that intonation may become flatter. Attention to these clues could explain some of my mother's success in spotting my lies as a child. She had the good fortune of knowing me well. There are two difficulties here. First, as Ekman (1997) points out, a truthful person who is thinking about a reply may show hesitation and lack fluency. Therefore, understanding the context and knowing how well the person understands the topic would be important in detecting a lie. To recognise these clues successfully without training would require a close relationship with the person.

Physical signs are another way to recognise lies. For example, Ekman (1997) notes that an averting of a gaze or a lessening of hand motions as people speak can be clues to lying. When people are lying, they often hide their true emotions and may exhibit what is called "leakage" (Ekman & Friesen, 1969). This means that signs of the hidden emotion leak out. For example, if people find something distasteful and lie by saying that the object in question is lovely, their smile may appear tight or strained. Once again, recognising lies using these clues must be done with care. Many people who are nervous may exhibit similar behaviours. Ekman concludes that the person who recognises lies with a fair amount of accuracy assesses emotions, is aware of what behaviours to zero in on, and is observant of these physical clues.

If there are definite clues that can be identified, why are we so easily duped by liars? From the above, it is obvious that a knowledge of the person is necessary or at least helpful. We do not always have such a close knowledge of the person who is lying to us. However, even those to whom we are very close can deceive us. Ekman (1997) says that we often rely on what is said and ignore the expressive behaviours. This means that we may miss many of the important clues given by a person who is lying. Also, we may collude with the liar, perhaps because we do not want to know that we are being lied to. This could be true, for example, for situations in which a person is covering up adultery. A wife may want to believe the lie rather than think that her husband is betraying her.

It appears then that recognising lies is a difficult task but not impossible. It requires a real desire to know the truth and a knowledge of what to look for. My mother wanted to raise an honest child. It was important to her to catch me if I lied so as to be able to teach me not to do it. She knew me well and desired to know the truth. That is not always the case with us, so we frequently do not recognise lies.

References

Ekman, P. (1997). Lying and Deception. In Stein, N.L., Ornstein, P. A., Tversky, B., & Brainerd, C. (1997) *Memory for Everyday and Emotional Events*. Mahwah, N.J.: Lawrence Erlbaum Associates.

Ekman, P. & Friesen, W.V. (1969). Nonverbal leakage and clues to deception. *Psychiatry* 32, 88-105.

| Activity 6 | Comprehension Check and Discussion |

Work with a partner to find answers for the following questions:
1. What are the main points in the above essay?
2. Do you agree with her ideas? Explain.
3. How does this essay affect your earlier assumptions about recognising lies?
4. Earlier you wrote a definition of *lies*. How does this author's definition differ from yours? What might you want to add to or change in your earlier definition?

3. Purpose, Audience, and Topic

The above activities have encouraged you to think about the general topic of lies. In the following, you will organise your ideas so that you can write your own research paper.

Activity 7	Choosing and Narrowing a Topic

Before you can develop this general topic in more detail for your research paper, you need to be clear about three specific questions:

PURPOSE: What is the purpose of your paper?
AUDIENCE: Who is the audience for your paper?
TOPIC: What is the precise topic of your paper?

a) Purpose

What is the *purpose* of your research paper? That is, what do you want it to do? Research papers tend to follow a specific organisation, and the language used in them is likely to be more formal than most other types of writing. Your paper might summarise current research; it might show that there is a flaw in current research; or it might report a recent development, etc.

Write some ideas on the *purpose* of your paper: _____

_____

b) Audience

Who is your *audience*? That is, who is going to read your research paper? You need to have a clear sense of your audience in order to provide appropriate information and details in your paper. If your anticipated audience consists of experts on the topic, for example, you would not likely give basic background information about the topic. On the other hand, if your audience consists of individuals who have no background on the topic, you would give them enough to enable them to understand the issues you develop.

Write down some notes about the *audience* for your paper: _____

_____

c) Topic

How are you going to focus your *topic*? You are going to work with the general topic of *Lies*—but how are you going to narrow it down to a manageable size? Once you have determined the focus of your paper, you can formulate a tentative thesis statement and work out a preliminary outline for your material.

Write down some notes on the *topic* of your paper: _____

_____

_____

Finding answers to these questions will help you to think carefully about the direction you want to take in your paper. Your answers to the PAT Principle and the ideas you developed in Activity 3 should allow you to decide which specific research question(s) you want to pursue in your paper. The research question(s) you identify will help you stay focussed as you develop your ideas in your paper.

4. Developing Research Questions

What are the questions you expect to answer in your paper? Think of some tentative questions that you might research, and then select the most appropriate one. Remember that it may be helpful to identify one major question and then some smaller, related ones.

Tentative research questions: _____

_____

_____

Arrange to go to the library to find some sources on "lies" for your research. If necessary, arrange to get the help of a librarian to show you how to start. You should find two to four sources that will give you additional ideas. You will need to cite one or two of these sources in your paper.

For an introduction to research in the library, consult *Library Skills* in the Resource Centre, pages 175-176.

Activity 8	Thesis Statement

Take a few minutes to think about a possible thesis statement. Then write it in the space below:

Working thesis statement: _____

_____

Working with two or three peers, follow each of these steps:
1. Read each other's thesis statement.
2. Discuss what main ideas could be developed for each thesis statement.
3. Suggest how each might need to be modified to make it more appropriate.
4. Finally, read some of the thesis statements to the whole class and listen carefully to the ones being read out by your peers.

5. Preparing to Write the First Draft

Before you can write the first draft, you need to collect and organise all your ideas about the topic. One technique writers use for this consists of writing notecards. This is the technique you will try in Activity 9.

1. Get some notecards ready. You will need several cards in at least five different colours—one each for your
   - thesis statement
   - main ideas
   - supporting ideas
   - quotations, paraphrases
   - references

2. Select the thesis statement you want to work with and write it on a notecard. Treat it as "a work in progress" and refine it as you get to know your topic better.

3. Select a second coloured notecard. Write each main idea you plan to use in your paper on a separate card of the same colour.

4. On a third coloured notecard, record the supporting ideas you plan to use. Use one card for each supporting idea.

5. Select notecards of a fourth colour and carefully note the exact quotations and passages for paraphrases. Again, each passage needs to be on a separate card.

6. Use the fifth colour of your notecards to write down the full reference of each source you plan to use for your paper. List each source on a separate card. Although you should have several cards with different sources, you may decide not to include more than two sources in your final draft.

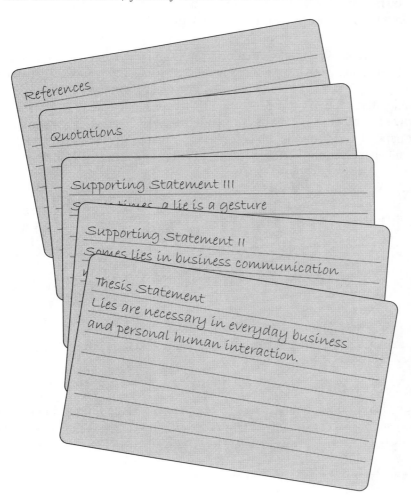

References

Quotations

Supporting Statement III
Sometimes a lie is a gesture

Supporting Statement II
Somes lies in business communication

Thesis Statement
Lies are necessary in everyday business
and personal human interaction.

7. When you have prepared some cards for each section, organise them into a coherent sequence. Try several different sequences until you find one that you like. Note how the different colours help you organise the main components of your research paper and how the card system allows you to change the sequence quickly and easily. You can accommodate additional material or discard material you no longer consider relevant. As you find additional support for your main ideas through your research, you can add new cards. The card system allows you to determine quickly whether you have enough "ideas" for each of the different sections. Remember to copy each quotation you may wish to use on a separate card and to ensure that you have a card with all the bibliographic details for the reference section. Refer back to Unit 6 if you need a reminder of how to deal with references.

Outlines provide a framework or skeleton of a paper. They show how the topic is divided into more important and less important subsections. Some writers like to make an outline before they start writing their paper, while others prefer to write a first draft and then create an outline to check the logical progression of ideas and the completeness of the arguments they wish to make. For this paper, write your outline before you write your paper.

Activity 10   Preparing an Outline

When you think that you have most of the main and supporting ideas you want to discuss in your paper, and you are satisfied with the sequence you worked out in Activity 9, Step 7, prepare your outline.

Below is an example of different levels of ideas that could appear in an outline. Note that the Roman numerals (I, II, III, IV, V, etc.) show the most important ideas that will be covered. Subdivisions use block or capital letters (A, B, C, D, etc.). Additional subdivisions, if necessary, use Arabic numerals (1, 2, 3, etc.) and small letters (a, b, c, etc.). Make sure that your numbers and letters are sequential and lined up below each other. Whether or not you include this numbering system in the text when you write your paper depends on the subject area. For example, English papers rarely include numbered subtitles while papers in the social sciences and in business usually do.

SAMPLE OUTLINE

I. _____

    A. _____

    B. _____

    C. _____

II. _____

    A. _____

    B. _____

        1. _____

        2. _____

3. _____

4. _____

C. _____

  1. _____

  2. _____

    a. _____

    b. _____

    c. _____

    d. _____

      (1) _____

      (2) _____

III. _____

IV. _____

A. _____

B. _____

Activity 11   **First Draft of Your Paper**

1. Use your outline to develop your notes into paragraphs and the paragraphs into sections.
2. Remember that each paragraph usually consists of one main idea expressed in a topic sentence, followed by sentences with supporting ideas and a concluding sentence.
3. Review relevant rhetorical structures in Part I if necessary.
4. Indicate clearly whether you are paraphrasing or quoting an author, and use some of the verbs and phrases you worked with in Unit 6.
5. Pay close attention to the way you help your reader(s) remember your thesis statement and refer to it again in your conclusions.

Revision is important even for professional writers. Revision provides an opportunity to move ideas around, add to the text, and to possibly delete material. Don't worry too much about specific questions you might have about standard grammar as you will work on these in a later activity. For the time being, concentrate on the clarity and completeness of your ideas and the sequence in which you present them. Writers use different revision techniques. In the following activity, you will use two of these for this research paper assignment.

Activity 12   **Revising Your First Draft**

Revision Technique A

1. Read your paper aloud carefully, several times if necessary.
2. Keep a pencil and paper at hand and write down any ideas, questions, or criticisms that occur to you while you read your paper.
3. Ask yourself questions as you read your paper. Here are some possible questions:
   a) Have you said everything you wanted to say?
   b) Did you support all your main points?
   c) Did you explain and develop your ideas clearly?
   d) Are your sources clearly indicated?

When you have made as many notes as you can, put your paper and the notes aside.

Revision Technique B

1. Ask a peer to read your paper and to give you general comments that might help you improve your draft. You might use the Peer Feedback Questions in the Resource Centre, page 172.
2. Write down questions about parts of your paper that you find difficult. Give these questions to your peer.
3. When you receive his or her feedback, read the notes carefully and ask for clarifications if necessary.

Revision Technique C

1. You now have notes on potential revisions from two different sources: your own reading and the feedback from a peer. Take the notes you produced and those from your peer.
2. Decide which points will improve your paper.
3. Incorporate those that suit the focus of your topic, your audience, and your purpose in writing this research paper.
4. Keep careful notes on the revisions you want to make in your final draft.

6. Editing and Final Copy

Once you have made all the revisions, your final draft needs careful editing. You have seen a number of different editing techniques by now and should follow those that are most appropriate for your writing style. An additional editing activity is suggested in Activity 13.

Activity 13   **Editing Your Final Copy**

Now that you have all your ideas on paper in an appropriate sequence, it is time to look closely at the grammar, vocabulary, spelling, punctuation, and presentation of your research paper. Note that many writers find this easier to do if they leave some time between completing the revision and the editing stages. If there is time,

1. Leave your paper for a day or two before you proceed to the editing stage.
2. Rephrase sentences as necessary to make them clearer or to add variety to the sentence constructions.
3. Check especially the logical connectors (e.g., *however, but, because*) you have used to express relationships between two ideas.
4. Look up their definition(s) in a good unilingual English dictionary if you have doubts about the meaning of certain words.
5. If you have access to a word processor with a spell checker, use the spell checker to correct any problems that might turn up. Otherwise, use a dictionary to check your spelling.
6. Ensure that the section numbers are in sequence, that the page numbers are in place, and that the reference section of your paper is complete and consistent with APA or your instructor's requirements.

It is customary to create a cover or title page for a research paper.

If your instructor does not have specific requirements for the cover page, follow the generic example in the Resource Centre. The following information is usually found on a cover page.
- Your name and student identification number
- The title of your paper
- The name and number of the course for which you submit the paper
- The name of your instructor
- The date of submission of your paper

LIES IN PERSPECTIVE

I. C. Green
Student ID 199 656 77
Course: ESL 455
Instructor: R. U. Right
April 1, 2002

When you have created your title page, select double spacing for the body of your paper, then print it out on paper and assemble it before you hand it in.

Summary of Real Life Writing Task 7
In this unit you
- analysed a sample paper
- used notecards to keep track of your ideas
- developed an outline
- wrote a first and at least one second draft of a research paper on "lies"
- quoted and paraphrased sources
- compiled your references
- created a cover page.

Alternate Topics
Other potential topics for a research paper include:
Employment
Globalisation
Lifestyle
Healthcare
Justice
Ethics
Morals

THE RESOURCE CENTRE
EDITING CHECKLIST

Item #	Description of Item to Check For	Date
1.	a subject and predicate verb in every sentence	02/05/08
2.	subject/verb agreement	02/05/08
3.	-s for 3rd person singular verbs in present tense	02/05/09

Suggested Items for Editing Checklist

Grammar: This category involves a large number of possible items, such as
- verb tense consistency
- inclusion of a subject and a predicate verb in each sentence
- subject/verb agreement
- appropriate use of adjective clauses and adverbial clauses
- appropriate use of transition elements
- standard word order–appropriate use of verb tenses; irregular forms where appropriate
- vocabulary that reflects intended meaning and level of formality

Additional items:
-
-
-
-

Mechanics:
- upper/lower case
- punctuation
- spelling (use spell checker on word processor whenever possible)
- page numbering
- format according to guidelines
- title page with required information (usually name of author, title, date, name of instructor, course number)

Text:
- consistency in titles, subtitles, and formatting features
- clear thesis/focus
- all paragraphs relevant to thesis/focus
- inclusion of introduction, body, and conclusion

Paragraphs:
- topic sentence giving main idea
- supporting sentences
- concluding sentence
- no unrelated ideas
- transitions between paragraphs

First Draft

The student's first draft of the paragraph as submitted to the teacher shows the teacher's comments.

Getting Ahead
Luo Lui

Most young people wants to get a university education. Because of there expectation of its

Good starting point !

effects on their future. Some think a university degree on a resume affects the kind of

consideration they will be given when applying for a job. Students think the social network is

Can you expand on this?

important. Students also see another effect as important. That is the variety of skills picked up

What skills? Try to be specific!

as a result of studying in any field that are transfaroble from situation to situation. These skills

learned in university can be used in any field of work.

Don't forget to add a concluding sentence.

Note that the instructor does not comment on grammar and mechanics.

The teacher asked students to discuss the feedback from her with a student and to explore ideas for improvement. This student has made improvements in the organisation and content. Now she has underlined errors in punctuation, grammar, and spelling so that his final draft will be the best he can make it.

Getting Ahead
Luo Lui

Most young people aspire to a university education. Because of there expectations of its effects on their future. First some think a university degree on a resume affects the kind of consideration they will be given when applying for a job. If a potential employer has a choice between a person with a university education and one without, they believe that the employer will choose the person with the degree. A second effect considered important to students is the social network of friends, professors, and employers who can influence our job search and make it more successful. Students also see a third effect as important. That is the variety of skills picked up as a result of studying in any field that are transfaroble from situation to situation. For example, in university students learn to read and select out the important material, to analyse and synthesise information, to write essays and reports, to critique ideas and research and to develop time management skills. These are just a few of the skills learned in university that can be used in any field of work. Understanding that these possible results of a university education widen their possibilities for future success leads many young people to compete for a place in a university program.

Good improvement; remember to proofread your work!

The final draft the student handed in looked like this:

Getting Ahead
Luo Lui

Most young people aspire to a university education because of their expectations of its effects on their future. First, some think a university degree on a resume affects the kind of consideration they will be given when applying for a job. If a potential employer has a choice between a person with a university education and one without, they believe that the employer will choose the person with the degree. A second effect considered important to students is the social network of friends, professors, and co-op employers who can influence their job search and make it more successful. Students also see a third effect as important. That is the variety of skills picked up as a result of studying in any field that are transferable from situation to situation. For example, in university students learn to read and select out the important material, to analyse and synthesise information, to write essays and reports, to critique ideas and research, and to develop time management skills. These are just a few of the skills learned in university that can be used in any field of work. Understanding that these possible results of a university education widen their possibilities for future success leads many young people to compete for a place in a university program.

THE RESOURCE CENTRE
PEER FEEDBACK QUESTIONS

Use only those questions your teacher indicates.

Read your partner's text, and then write notes for the following questions.

1. What is the writer's purpose?

2. What is the writer's thesis?

3. In a single paragraph text, circle the controlling idea. In a multi-paragraph text, underline the topic sentence in each paragraph.

4. How are the main ideas supported?

5. How did the writer introduce the topic?

Add any suggestions for improving the introduction:
6. How did the writer conclude?

Add any suggestions for improving the conclusion:
7. What part or parts of the text do you find difficult to understand?

8. Where do you think the writer should add more detail?

9. Are there specific words or expressions the writer might like to include?

10. Add any additional suggestions you may have.

Before you discuss your feedback with your partner, complete the sentence below:
What I liked most about this draft is...

THE RESOURCE CENTRE
PORTFOLIO WRITING

Your teacher may ask you to keep track of your writing assignments in a portfolio. The portfolio is a collection of your writing that includes notes, outlines, various drafts, and revisions. It contains a representative selection of your work and serves to show progress and achievements in your writing. When used in a writing course, the portfolio may be used as a form of assessment that actively involves the learners. Your writing portfolio gives a broad portrait of your writing performance over a period of time, often the length of a writing course.

A writing portfolio represents a collection as well as a selection of an individual writer's work. Although your teacher may specify the basic number and type of writing assignments to be included in your portfolio, you will likely write several additional assignments and in some cases, you may write drafts that reflect different approaches to the same assignment. You should carefully select the pieces of work you want to include in your portfolio, then explain your reasons for including each piece in comments you submit with your portfolio. For example, you may want to include a piece of your work because it reflects your best writing. However, a portfolio may also contain work that shows an individual's growth as a writer. You might include a piece of writing because an assignment presented a special challenge for you or because it illustrates a weakness you recognise in your writing. Your portfolio might then reflect how you have dealt with a challenging writing task, or how you have worked on developing specific writing skills to address a weakness. Be sure to include comments that explain your reasons for selecting the pieces you include in your portfolio. As you select the pieces of writing for your portfolio, you will need to reflect on the merits of each piece. In the process, you develop your ability to look at your work critically and identify strengths and weaknesses in your writing. Collecting and selecting work for your portfolio enables you to become an active participant in the learning process and its assessment.

On the next page is an example of a tracking sheet designed to record individual pieces of work in a writing portfolio. Depending on the number of assignments, you may need to use more than one tracking sheet. Give an abbreviated title or the topic for each assignment in the first column. Columns two to five reflect the dates when specific stages for individual assignments were completed. If you have not completed all the steps for an assignment, write *n/a* (not applicable) instead of the date. In column six, list the main points you learned or practised in the assignment (e.g., outlining, topic sentence, paragraph structure, describing a process, writing references). Alternately, you may write "See separate sheet" in the space, and then write "Comments" and the title of the assignment, followed by your comments, on a separate sheet.

Tracking Sheet

	Date 1st draft completed	Date revised to include teacher feedback	Date revised to include peer feedback	Date final draft edited	Focus of assignment (What I learned in this unit)	Teacher's final comments
Assignment 1:						
Assignment 2:						
Assignment 3:						
Assignment 4:						
Assignment 5:						
Assignment 6:						
Assignment 7:						
Assignment 8:						
Assignment 9:						
Assignment 10:						

THE RESOURCE CENTRE
LIBRARY SKILLS

Using the Library to Find Sources for Your Essay

1. Look up your topic in the online or card catalogue. Remember to use a reference book to identify terms that are used for your topic if you have a problem. Using different terms to access material is one way to find additional sources.

2. In the library, find a recent book about your topic. Skim through the book to answer the questions below.

3. Read the chapter topics in the table of contents to see which chapters may be useful to you. Use the index to check terms that relate to your topic. Check the footnotes or endnotes in the relevant chapters for other articles or books that are related to your topic. In some texts and most articles, the bibliography or references are at the end. Check there too for related material. Annotated bibliographies can be very helpful when you look for sources.

4. Check for tables, charts, and illustrations. Would they be helpful?

5. Ask yourself if the book you have in mind would be useful for your essay. What are the author's qualifications on the subject matter? If you answer yes, make notes or complete notecards about the following information. Include all the information about the book that would be necessary to list in your bibliography.

Author(s) or editor(s):_____

Title:_____

Place of publication:_____

Publisher:_____

Copyright date:_____

Number of pages: _____ Library call number _____ ISBN # _____

> **IMPORTANT: For a chapter in an edited text, you need to record the name of the author, the title, and the page numbers of the relevant chapter(s).**

6. Find a recent academic journal article about your topic. Use ERIC, PSYCHLIT, or another suitable database. Alternately, you can look in a journal index for your area of research. Write down the information necessary for both finding the article in the library and including it in your bibliography. The citation for a magazine article will include the following information:

Author: _____

Title of the article:_____

Date of the journal:_____

Magazine title:_____

Volume/number: _____ Page numbers:_____ Library Call number:_____

7. Make notes on the material as suggested in points 3 to 5 above.

IMPORTANT: Take note of useful information and the pages on which it is found, including short passages that you might want to use as quotations. Write down the information accurately, making sure that spelling and punctuation are exactly as they appear in the original. Always write down the page number. This information can be placed on your notecards as you work. Once you have outlined your essay and decided on topics for each paragraph, you can add the number of the relevant paragraph to your notes or notecards. Of course, you may not need to use all the sources gathered in your notes or notecards. You may decide later that some sources are not as pertinent to your research paper as you originally thought.

Example of a Reference List

The following is an example of a reference list, which usually starts on a separate page. Note that the information required for each source differs depending on whether the source is a book, a journal article, a report, an Internet source, or another document.

REFERENCES

American Psychological Association. (2001). *Publication manual of the American Psychological Association (5th edition)*. Washington, DC: American Psychological Association.

Horowitz, D. (1986). What professors actually require: Academic tasks for the ESL classroom. *TESOL Quarterly*, 20 (3), 445-462.

Land, B. (2001, July 1). *Web Extension to American Psychological Association Style (WEAPAS)* (Rev. 2.0) [WWW document; retrieved April 4, 2002]. URL http://www.beadsland.com/weapas/

Martin, N. (1983). Scope for intentions. In A. Freedman, I. Pringle, & J. Yalden (Eds.). *Learning to Write: First Language/Second Language* (pp. 207-218). London: Longman.

Nunan, D. (1991). *Language Teaching Methodology*. New York: Prentice Hall.

Raimes, A. (1983). What unskilled ESL students do as they write: A classroom study of composing. *TESOL Quarterly* 19 (2), 229-258.

Stepp-Greany, J. (2002). Student perceptions on language learning in a technological environment: Implications for the new millennium. *Language Learning & Technology*, Vol. 6, No.1, January 2002, 165-180.

Zamel, Vivian, & Spack, Ruth (Eds.). (1998). *Negotiating academic literacies: Teaching and learning across languages and cultures*. Mahwah, NJ: Erlbaum.

THE RESOURCE CENTRE
COVER PAGE

The cover page illustrated here reflects a generic format that can be used for most assignments. However, you should always check with your instructor first to find out if he or she has specific requirements.

Frequently required information to be listed includes:
- name of author
- if appropriate, student identification number
- title of paper/assignment
- course name and number
- name of instructor
- date of submission of paper

LIES IN PERSPECTIVE
I. C. Green
Student ID 199 656 77

Course: ESL 455
Instructor: R. U. Right
November 29, 2002

THE RESOURCE CENTRE
SELECTED WEB SITES

Internet addresses sometimes change or become unavailable. The addresses included in this section were checked before going to print.

Bibliographies

An example of an *Annotated Bibliography* is available from the Online Writing Lab (OWL), Purdue University, at
http://owl.english.perdue.edu/handouts/general/gl_annotatedbibEX.html

A bibliography on *Evaluating Internet Sources* is available from the Virginia Tech University Libraries at
http://www.lib.vt.edu/research/libinst/evalbiblio.html

A *Bibliography Styles Handbook* for APA and MLA format is available from the Writer's Workshop, University of Illinois at Urbana-Champaign is at
http://www.english.edu/cws/wworkshop/bibliostyles.htm

Concordancer

Cobuild/Collins Sampler
http://titania.cobuild.collins.co.uk/form.html

Electronic Style Guides

The University of Wisconsin-Madison Writing Center
APA
http://www.wisc.edu/writing/Handbook/DocAPA1.html

MLA
http://www.wisc.edu/writing/Handbook/DocMLA.html

Chicago/Turabian
http://www.wisc.edu/writing/Handbook/DocChicago.html

Writing Centres and Grammar Help

Charles Darling's Guide to Grammar and Writing, Capital Community College
http://webster.commnet.edu/grammar/index.htm

Longman resources
http://www.longman.com/grammarexpress
http://www.longman.com/grammarexchange
http://www.longman.com/webdictionary

On-line Writing Centre, OWL at Purdue University
http://owl.english.purdue.edu/handouts/esl/eslstudent.html

Writing at the University of Toronto
http://www.utoronto.ca/writing/advise.html

University of St. Thomas' ISS-Learning Center
Writing the five-paragraph essay and other writing tips; Style Guides; Grammar and other Resources
http://www.iss.stthomas.edu/studyguides/bib_writing.htm

Additional Web Sites:

_____

_____

_____

_____

THE RESOURCE CENTRE
TRANSITIONS

Transitions (also called connectors or connecting words) are used to hold sentences and paragraphs together so that every sentence in a paragraph and every paragraph in an essay become an integral part of the whole. This coherence is also maintained by the organisation of ideas in a logical order and the structure of the paragraph or essay. Transitions lead the reader through your argument. They are oftenassociated with particular organisational patterns such as comparison/contrast, describing a process,giving directions, or cause/effect. Remember that coherence (holding the ideas together) is also achieved through pronoun reference, demonstratives, and repetition. Having too many transition words can be awkward.

Addition

and	another	similarly	moreover
furthermore	in addition	too	also
equally important	next	finally	first
second	besides	likewise	in the same way

Cause and Effect

consequently	if...then	as a result	because
since	therefore	as an effect	for that reason

Chronology

Sequence or time

when	immediately	upon (e.g., after seeing something)	
since	first	next	earlier
meanwhile	at the same time	in the meantime	soon afterward
afterwards	subsequently	later	

Beginning of a sequence

first of all	in the beginning	at first	at the start

Middle

next	when	immediately	upon
since then	after that	then	second
third	following	subsequently	earlier
meanwhile	in the meantime	soon afterward	afterwards
later			

End

eventually	at last	in the end	finally

Clarification/Explanation:
in other words, for example, for instance

Comparison:
both, each, in the same way, similarly, likewise, correspondingly

Concession:
naturally, granted, of course, though, to be sure, although, despite, in spite of, for all that, while, to be sure

Conclusion and Explanation:
therefore, thus, then, consequently, as a consequence, as a result, accordingly, finally, for this/these reasons, on that account, because of, because, so, since, in conclusion, to sum up, as has been noted, all in all

Contrast:
but, however, still, nevertheless, on the one hand/on the other hand, on the contrary, by contrast, in contrast, yet, although, while, in spite of, despite, whereas

Emphasis:
(to show that one idea is more important than the others): above all, especially, most important

Explanation/Illustration:
for example, to illustrate, by way of illustration, to be specific, specifically, in particular, thus, for instance, in other words, in fact, as a matter of fact, namely

Location:
nearby, beside, above, below, in front of, beyond, to the right of, to the left of, under, over

THE RESOURCE CENTRE
COMMON ERRORS

This section lists some common errors and is intended as a brief summary for students who have experience with English grammar. For more details, students should consult a grammar text.

Explanation of symbols: √ = appropriate/standard English

X = inappropriate/non-standard English

? = questionable or ambiguous construction

Agreement

refers to the use of words of like number and gender; two distinct areas of agreement are discussed below. See **Pronoun-Antecedent** agreement and **Subject-Verb** agreement.

Ambiguous modifier

refers to a misplaced modifier or a squinting modifier; a modifier that could relate to two or more references.

? The police officer looked at the boy with binoculars.
("*with binoculars*" could modify "*looked*" or "*boy*")

√ The police officer used binoculars to look at the boy with binoculars.
(possible correction)

Articles

are used in English to let readers know if an object or idea being discussed is a specific item or not. Articles are complex and require careful attention to avoid omissions or inappropriate use. Check for the following:
When you

1. introduce an idea or object, you use the indefinite article "*a*":

√ On vacation, Fred likes to read a good book.

2. use the definite article *the*, you refer to a specific idea or object:

√ The book has to offer adventure, mystery, and suspense.

3. do not need an article (also called *zero* or *0* article).

√ Books his friends have recommended in the past have often disappointed him.

✓   Balancing work and leisure can be difficult.

4.   have already introduced a subject in an earlier sentence, the definite article *"the"* is likely required.

✓   While on vacation, the mayor read many books. The book he liked best dealt with drug smuggling and corruption.

Capitalisation
refers to the use of upper-case letters for the first word in new sentences and proper names.

Case
refers to the inflected form taken by a noun or pronoun to show its relationship to other words.

X   The students received <u>his</u> grades two weeks after the last day of classes. (non-standard)

✓   The students received <u>their</u> grades two weeks after the last day of classes. (corrected)

Choppy sentences
are found in paragraphs that use a series of very short, basic sentences. The writing seems *"choppy"* or *"abrupt"*.

X   Bangkok is a rapidly developing city. It is located near the Gulf of Thailand. It is a very large city. Many people live in the city. It has serious traffic congestion. Bangkok has many tourist attractions. It is worth visiting. (choppy sentences)

Choppy sentences are best avoided through sentence combining. Analyse the sentences, look for relationships between the ideas, and then combine the sentences while removing unnecessary material.

✓   Bangkok, near the Gulf of Thailand, is a large and rapidly developing city with a large population. Despite its serious traffic congestion, its many tourist attractions are worth visiting. (corrected)

Collective noun
refers to a noun that is singular in form but represents a collection of individuals (e.g., army, committee, crowd, team); it is treated as a singular noun when the collection is thought of as a whole but may be treated as a plural when the individual members are thought of as acting separately.

✓   The committee was unanimous in its decision to oust the president. (one unit)

✓   The committee were divided on the issue of replacing the president. (a group of individuals)

Comma fault
See Comma splice.

Comma splice

results from joining two main clauses with a comma. Instead, use a semicolon or a comma and a coordinating conjunction (also called a comma fault or fused sentence).

X   Library research is an important part of writing a research paper, it can take up a lot of time. (comma splice)

√   Library research is an important part of writing a research paper that can take up a lot of time. (corrected)

√   Library research is an important part of writing a research paper; it can take up a lot of time. (corrected)
See Semicolon, in punctuation section.

Comparative

is a form of an adjective or adverb showing a greater, but not the greatest, degree in meaning, usually indicated by the suffix _-er_ (cheaper) or by the use of _more_ (more expensive); it is used to compare two objects or ideas.

The comparative form is usually used when comparing two items:

√   Self-employed individuals are likely to work longer hours than those employed by a public or private company.

Compound object

exists when two or more direct or indirect objects following a verb or a verb form require a plural verb form.

X   According to recent research, fruit and vegetables is important for a healthy diet. (non-standard)

√   According to recent research, fruit and vegetables are important components of a healthy diet. (corrected)

Compound predicate

is formed when a subject may have two or more predicates (verbs).

√   The leaders of the team tried to motivate and encourage their team members.

Compound subjects

are found when sentences contain two or more subjects.

√   Researching sources and developing ideas are important components of writing an academic paper.

Dangling modifier

is a modifier that has no clear reference. Errors in logic occur when writers do not make the intended meaning clear, as the following examples show (also called misplaced modifiers).

?   Working in the library, the computer was useful.
    (It sounds like the computer worked in the library.)

√   As the students were working in the library, they found the computer useful. (corrected)

?   The unhappy students were seen by the professor marking the assignments.
    (It appears that the students were marking the assignments.)

√   The unhappy students were seen by the professor as he was marking the assignments.
    (Corrected)

Dependent clause

refers to a clause that cannot stand alone as a standard sentence but depends on a main clause for its meaning (also called a *subordinate clause*).

X   Although the director called the meeting. (dependent clause; incomplete sentence)

√   Although the director called the meeting, he had no intention of attending it. (corrected)

Direct object

is a noun or noun phrase that shows who or what receives the action of a transitive verb.

X   Professor Smith repeated. (non-standard: a transitive verb requires a direct object)

√   Professor Smith repeated the special lecture on human cloning.
    (The noun phrase *special lecture on human cloning* receives the action of the action expressed in the verb *repeated*.)

Faulty parallelism

occurs when different sentence structures are used in a list of two or more items connected with a conjunction (e.g., *and*).

X   When consumers buy used cars, they look for low cost, it should run well, and low mileage. (faulty parallelism)

√   When consumers buy used cars, they look for low cost, good running order, and low mileage. (corrected)

X   To use a computer and accessing databases are part of the daily routine for many librarians. (non-standard)

√   Using computers and accessing databases are part of the daily routine for many librarians. (corrected)

Fragment (of a sentence)

is an incomplete sentence used as if it were complete but lacks a subject or verb.

X   *Returning repeatedly to the library for information.* (incomplete, subject missing)

√   *Returning repeatedly to the library for information, the students finally had the data they needed to write their research paper.* (corrected, subject *the students* added)

Fused sentence

See Comma splice.

Independent clause

refers to a group of words, containing a subject and a main verb, that can stand alone (also called a main clause, or a sentence)

X   *Writing quickly, completed the test within the two hours allowed.* (no subject, non-standard)

X   *Writing quickly, the students the test within the two hours allowed.* (no main verb, non-standard)

√   *Writing quickly, the students completed the test within the two hours allowed.* (corrected)

Irregular verb

is a verb that does not follow the regular *-ed* ending pattern for past and past participle forms.

X   *The new students seeked the professor's advice on how to catch up with their course readings.* (non-standard)

√   *The new students sought the professor's advice on how to catch up with their course readings.* (corrected)

Main clause

refers to a group of words, containing a subject and a main verb, that can stand alone (also called an independent clause, or a sentence).

X   *Writing quickly, completed the test within the two hours allowed.* (no subject, non-standard)

X   *Writing quickly, the students the test within the two hours allowed.* (no main verb, non-standard)

√   *Writing quickly, the students completed the test within the two hours allowed.* (corrected)

Misplaced modifiers

See Dangling modifiers.

Modal verbs

are auxiliary verbs. Few of them can be used with a *"to"* infinitive and they do not allow tense and person markers.

X   The chemistry professor could to perform the experiment. (non-standard)

√   The chemistry professor could perform the experiment. (corrected)

X   The student can goes to the library to get copies of previous exam scripts. (non-standard)

√   The student can go to the library to get copies of previous exam scripts. (corrected)

Parallel structure
See Faulty parallelism.

Passive voice

is the voice or form of a verb whose subject is the object or receiver of the action of the verb. Although passive voice is often overused, it may be appropriate for two types of situations:

1.   When the agent (doer) of an action is not known or not important, e.g.,

√   The two chemicals were mixed and added to the serum. (agent not important)

√   The earliest of these buildings was built at the turn of the century. (agent not known)

√   Smith was voted most accomplished athlete of the year. (agent not important)

2.   When the writer does not want to name the agent, perhaps because the information is not popular, e.g.,

√   Valuable equipment was stolen or damaged during the riots.

√   The increase in salaries and benefits for employees was not approved.

Possessive

is often expressed through an apostrophe with singular (*'s*) and plural (*s'*) nouns.

X   Marketing specialists influence consumer's spending habits through carefully designed advertising campaigns. (non-standard)

X   Marketing specialists influence consumers spending habits through carefully designed advertising campaigns. (non-standard)

√   Marketing specialists influence consumers' spending habits through carefully designed advertising campaigns.(corrected)

Prepositions

refer to a word or word group that connects a noun or pronoun, or a noun phrase, to another noun (the cost *of* living), to a verb (he wrote *to* the bank), or to an adjective (she was late *for* class).

Pronoun-Antecedent agreement

a pronoun should agree in number and gender with its antecedent (the word, phrase, or clause to which the pronoun refers)

X   The most recent council meetings have been well-attended. Each time, its agenda was published in the local media. (non-standard)

√   The most recent council meetings have been well-attended. Each time, their agenda was published in the local media. (corrected)

Some rules that apply to formal writing:

1. Pronouns ending in *one* or *body* are singular and require a singular verb or possessive.

    √   Everyone must hand in their composition by the end of this week. (informal)

    √   Everyone must hand in his or her composition by the end of this week. (formal)

2. Phrases between the subject and the verb in a sentence do not change the number of the subject.

    X   One of the new banking laws are difficult to enforce. (non-standard)

    √   One of the new banking laws is difficult to enforce. (corrected)

    √   The new building is across the street from a bank and a hotel. (standard)

    X   Across from the new building is a bank and a hotel. (non-standard)

    √   Across from the new building are a bank and a hotel. (standard)

3. Subject pronouns should not take the place of object pronouns.

    X   The supervisor congratulated Fred and I on a job well done. (non-standard)

    √   The supervisor congratulated Fred and me on a job well done. (corrected)

4. In informal conversations, native speakers of English sometimes use *myself* (i.e., the reflexive pronoun) in place of *me*. Use reflexive pronouns only where the context requires them:

    √   Fred pushed himself to finish the race in record time.

5. In formal English, *who* is used as a subject pronoun, and *whom* as the object of a verb or preposition. However, *who* is frequently used in these positions and *whom* is becoming rare.

√ Who gave the lecture on human cloning? He/she gave the lecture on human cloning. (*who* represents the subject)

√ Whom did the committee identify as the recipient of the award? The committee identified Mr. X as the recipient of the award. (*whom* represents the object of the verb)

√ To whom should the letter be addressed? The letter should be addressed to the council. (*to whom* represents the object of the preposition)

Run-on sentences

occur when two main clauses are joined in a non-standard manner. Two main clauses could be separated by a colon to form two separate sentences, but this technique may result in choppy sentences. Alternately, two main clauses can often be joined with a conjunction (*and*, *or*, *but*) to form a compound sentence. Finally, run-on sentences might be changed into a main and a subordinate clause, linked with a transition word, to form a complex sentence.

X The crew members had worked many extra hours they were exhausted. (run-on sentence)

√ The crew members had worked many extra hours. They were exhausted. (corrected)

√ The crew members had worked many extra hours and they were exhausted. (corrected)

√ The crew members had worked so many extra hours that they were exhausted. (corrected)

X The auction was very successful, it raised almost half a million dollars for cancer research. (run-on sentence)

√ The auction was very successful. It raised almost half a million dollars for cancer research. (corrected)

√ The auction was very successful and (it) raised almost half a million dollars for cancer research. (corrected)

√ The auction was very successful as it raised almost half a million dollars for cancer research. (corrected)

√ The auction was so successful that it raised almost half a million dollars for cancer research. (corrected)

Sentence

refers to a group of words, containing a subject and a main verb, that can stand alone (also called an independent clause or a main clause).

X Writing quickly, completed the test within the two hours allowed. (no subject non standard)

X   Writing quickly, the students the test within the two hours allowed. (no main verb, non-standard)

√   Writing quickly, the students completed the test within the two hours allowed. (corrected)

Sentence fragment

is an incomplete sentence used as a sentence in a written text. A sentence without a subject or verb is a sentence fragment. Also, a dependent clause used as a sentence results in a sentence fragment:

X   If the company treated its employees better. (sentence fragment). They would be in better spirits.

The first part is a dependent clause and incomplete as a sentence. If used on its own, the second part, although grammatically correct, would leave readers guessing who "they" refers to.

√   If the company treated its employees better, they would be in better spirits. (corrected)

Dependent clauses may contain a subject and a verb, but they do not express a complete thought.

X   Although the exams were difficult. (sentence fragment) The students finished their studies successfully.

√   Although the exams were difficult, the students finished their studies successfully. (corrected)

X   When new developments are first published in medical journals. (sentence fragment) The media tend to simplify their implications.

√   When new developments are first published in medical journals, the media tend to simplify their implications. (corrected)

Split infinitive

results from the separation of the marker _to_ from the verbal form of the infinitive. Although split infinitives are very frequent in oral language, they are often considered undesirable in formal writing.

?   When the situation became clear, the director decided to quickly call another meeting. (split infinitive)

√   When the situation became clear, the director decided to call another meeting quickly. (corrected)

Subject-Verb agreement

refers to agreement in number and person between subject and verb.

X *The bank rate are adjusted regularly.* (lack of subject-verb agreement within a sentence)

subject   verb
singular   plural

√ The bank rate is adjusted regularly. (corrected)

X Many students spend their summer working to save up for his tuition when he returns to classes in September. (lack of subject-pronoun agreement within a sentence)

√ Many students spend their summer working to save up for their tuition when they return to classes in September. (corrected)

X Many students spend their summer working. He needs the money to return to classes for another academic year. (lack of subject-verb agreement across sentences)

√ Many students spend their summer working. They need the money to return to classes for another academic year. (corrected)

Subjunctive mood (also called unreal conditional)

is the mood of a verb; used to express qualities like supposition, desire, or possibility, as opposed to actual fact.

X If I was in your place, I would apply to a graduate program. (non-standard)

√ If I were in your place, I would apply to a graduate program. (standard)

Subordinate clause

is a clause that cannot stand alone as a standard sentence but depends on a main clause for its meaning (also called a dependent clause).

X Although the director called the meeting. (subordinate clause, incomplete sentence)

√ Although the director called the meeting he had no intention of attending it. (corrected)

Superlative degree

is a form of adjective or adverb that shows the greatest degree in meaning. It is usually shown by the suffix -*est* (cheapest) or the use of *most* (most expensive). Note that the superlative is used when comparing more than two objects or ideas.

X   The busiest of the two students works ten hours a day in addition to studying full time. (non-standard)

√   The busiest of all the students works ten hours a day in addition to studying full time. (corrected)

or

√   The busier of the two students works ten hours a day in addition to studying full time. (corrected)

Tense shifts

occur when the tense changes within a sentence or a paragraph. Where there is no reason for a shift, the intended meaning becomes unclear.

X   When office computers were first introduced, administrators think that they will reduce the amount of paper used in offices. (tense shift)

√   When office computers were first introduced, administrators thought that they would reduce the amount of paper used in offices. (corrected)

Transitive verb

refers to a verb that requires a direct object to complete its meaning.

X   Once they had completed their first drafts, the students compared. (non-standard)

√   Once they had completed their first drafts, the students compared them. (corrected)

Wordiness

occurs when writers use too many words to describe an idea. Wordiness may also occur when sentences are too long and complex.

?   Successful students do well because they are careful to make sure that they plan and organise their time for their study assignments before they start so that they can make the most of the time that is available to them. (wordy)

An analysis of the sentence shows that many words and phrases are unnecessary. They repeat ideas. Eliminating unnecessary or repetitive words leaves the core idea:

√   Successful students plan their time efficiently. (corrected)

Word order

Words in an English sentence follow the *Subject-Verb-Object* (SVO) pattern.

√   Employment rates   reflect   the economic health of a country.

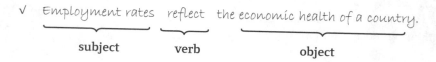

subject   **verb**   **object**

Word order involving adverbs

Note some typical adverb placements:

√ They deliver the supplies to the warehouse on Tuesdays. (Not: ...*on Tuesdays to the warehouse.*)

√ Members of an orchestra played quietly during the intermission.
(Not...*during the intermission quietly*)

√ The new student speaks English very well. (Not...*very well English*)

√ Can the professor meet with me now? (Not...*meet now with me*)

√ He has probably forgotten the appointment. (Not...*forgotten probably*)

Word order involving adjectives is complex, especially as exceptions occur. Here are some general rules:

1. Colour, origin/place, material and purpose precede other adjectives.

other	→	colour	→	origin/place	→	material	purpose
old		blue		Dresden		china	plates

Old blue Dresden china plates reach high prices at auctions all over the world.

soft	red	ostrich	feather	hats

Soft red ostrich feather hats are fashionable again.

2. Opinions tend to come before descriptions:

opinion	→	description	→	object

beautiful	old	building

A beautiful old building was demolished to make room for a highway.

opinion	→	description	→	description	object

useless	rusty	copper	pipes

The useless rusty copper pipes in the house were replaced with new ones.

3. *"First"* and *"last"* usually come before numbers:
the first three weeks (Not: the three first weeks)

THE RESOURCE CENTRE
A BRIEF GUIDE TO PUNCTUATION

This section is intended as a brief summary for students who have prior experience with punctuation and grammar. For more details, consult a textbook on punctuation.

At the end of a sentence

Periods are used at the end of simple sentences, compound sentences, and complex sentences.

Simple sentence: *Her research is biased.*

Compound sentence: *Her research is biased and fails to take several factors into account.*

Complex sentence: *Her research is biased because she did not consider the British results.*

Question marks are used at the end of a question.

Did the business do well last year?

Exclamation marks are used to show an emotional or emphatic utterance, usually in imaginative writing. They are used rarely, if at all, in academic writing.

Within sentences

Commas may come at the end of a phrase, after adverbs at the beginning of a sentence, at the end of a clause, or in lists.

After eating dinner, they went to the movies. (After a phrase)

Therefore, she disregarded the evidence. (After an adverb at the beginning of a sentence)

Because the evidence was weak, they decided to do a study with more subjects. (After a subordinate clause)

Joanne collected the material, and she tested it in the lab. (After an independent clause)

To examine mollusks you need tweezers, a clamp, and a pair of pliers. (In a list)

Semicolons are used with some transitions, or between independent clauses that are closely related in content/meaning.

The book was excellent; however, few people have read it. (With a transition word, notice the transition word is followed by a comma.)

It would also be possible to punctuate this type of transition word in the following way:

The book was excellent. However, few people have read it.

The accident caused a great problem; people were without water for five days. (Two closely related independent clauses–this usage is rare. Periods are used most often in such a case.)

The report included a short, succinct summary; broad, general guidelines; specific, clearly defined suggestions. (Used to separate items in a series that contains internal commas.)

Colons are used to direct the reader's attention forward, usually because what follows explains or develops what has just been said. Frequently what follows is a list.

Canadian writers have become renowned for many types of writing: poetry, novels, biographies, and autobiographies.

THE RESOURCE CENTRE
LIST OF IRREGULAR VERBS IN ENGLISH

For compound forms (e.g., _withdraw_), look for the single form (e.g., _draw_). If a verb has two possible forms and one is heard less frequently than the other, the less frequent one is given in _italics_. Both forms in regular print indicate that the forms are used interchangeably. If two forms involve two different meanings, they are marked with an asterisk(*). Select the intended meaning with the help of a good dictionary.

Base Form	Past Form	Participle Form	Base Form	Past Form	Participle Form
A			burst	burst	burst
arise	arose	arisen	buy	bought	bought
awake	awoke/ awaked	awoke/ _awaked_	**C**		
			cast	cast	cast
B			catch	caught	caught
be	was	been	chide	chid	chidden
bear	bore	borne/born*	choose	chose	chosen
beat	beat	beaten	clothe	clothed/clad	clothed/clad
become	became	become	come	came	come
befall	befell	befallen	cost	cost	cost
beget	begot	begotten	creep	crept	crept
begin	began	begun	crow	crowed/_crew_	crowed
behold	beheld	beheld	cut	cut	cut
bend	bent	bent			
bereave	bereaved	bereaved/bereft*	**D**		
beseech	besought	besought	deal	dealt	dealt
bet	bet	bet	dig	dug	dug
bid ("command")	bid	bidden	do	did	done
bid ("offer")	bid	bid	draw	drew	drawn
bind	bound	bound	dream	dreamt/ dreamed	dreamt/ dreamed
bite	bit	bitten	drink	drank	drunk
bleed	bled	bled	drive	drove	driven
blow	blew	blown	dwell	_dwelled/_ dwelt	dwelled/ dwelt
break	broke	broken			
bring	brought	brought			
broadcast	broadcast	broadcast			
build	built	built			
burn	burned	burnt			

Base Form	Past Form	Participle Form	Base Form	Past Form	Participle Form
E			knit ("unite," "draw together")**	knit	knit
eat	ate	eaten	know	knew	known
F			**L**		
fall	fell	fallen	lay	laid	laid
feed	fed	fed	lead	led	led
feel	felt	felt	lean	leaned/ leant	leaned/ leant
fight	fought	fought	leap	leaped/ leapt	leaped/ leapt
find	found	found	learn	learned/ learnt	learned/ learnt
flee	fled	fled			
fling	flung	flung	leave	left	left
fly	flew	flown	lend	lend	lent
forbear	forbore	forborne	let	let	let
forbid	forbade	forbidden	lie	lay	lain
forget	forgot	forgotten	light	lighted/lit	lit/lighted
forgive	forgave	forgiven	lose	lost	lost
forsake	forsook	forsaken			
freeze	froze	frozen	**M**		
			make	made	made
G			mean	meant	meant
get	got	got	meet	met	met
gild	gilded/gilt	gilded/gilt	mow	mowed	mowed/mown
give	gave	given			
go	went	gone	**P**		
grind	ground	ground	pay	paid	paid
grow	grew	grown	put	put	put
			prove	proved	proven/proved
H			put	put	put
hang	hung	hanged*/hung			
have	had	had	**R**		
hear	heard	heard	read	read	read
hew	hewed	hewed/hewn	rid	rid	rid
hide	hid	hidden	ride	rode	ridden
hit	hit	hit	ring	rang	rung
hold	held	held	rise	rose	risen
hurt	hurt	hurt	run	ran	run
K					
keep	kept	kept			
kneel	knelt	knelt			

*to knit as in "making garments from wool" is a regular verb

Base Form	Past Form	Participle Form	Base Form	Past Form	Participle Form
S			spread	spread	spread
saw	sawed	sawed/sawn	spring	sprang	sprung
say	said	said	stand	stood	stood
see	saw	seen	steal	stole	stolen
seek	sought	sought	stick	stuck	stuck
sell	sold	sold	sting	stung	stung
send	sent	sent	stink	stank/stunk	stunk
set	set	set	stride	strode	stridden
sew	sewed	sewed/sewn	strike	struck	struck
shake	shook	shaken	string	strung	strung
shave	shaved	shaved/shaven	strive	strove	striven
shear	sheared/	sheared/	swear	swore	sworn
	shore	shorn	sweep	swept	swept
shed	shed	shed	swell	swelled	swelled/swollen
shine	shone	shone	swim	swam	swum
shoot	shot	shot	swing	swung	swung
show	showed	showed/shown			
shrink	shrank	shrunk	**T**		
shut	shut	shut	take	took	taken
sing	sang	sung	teach	taught	taught
sink	sank	sunk	tear	tore	torn
sit	sat	sat	tell	told	told
slay	slew	slain	think	thought	thought
sleep	slept	slept	throw	threw	thrown
slide	slid	slid	thrust	thrust	thrust
sling	slung	slung	tread	trod	trodden/trod
slink	slunk	slunk			
slit	slit	slit	**U**		
smell	smelled/	smelled/	understand	understood	understood
	smelt	smelt			
sow	sowed	sowed/sown	**W**		
speak	spoke	spoken	wake	waked/woke/	waked/woken
speed	speeded/	speeded/	wear	wore	worn
	sped	sped	weave	wove	woven
spell	spelled/	spelled/	weep	wept	wept
	spelt	spelt	wet	wetted/wet	wetted/wet
spend	spent	spent	win	won	won
spill	spilled/spilt	spilled/spilt	wind	wound	wound
spin	spun	spun	wring	wrung	wrung
spit	spat	spat	write	wrote	written
split	split	split			

GLOSSARY

The definitions below refer to the way in which the terms are used in this text. Some words and phrases may have additional meanings. Please consult a dictionary for additional definitions.

A

abstract
writing that lacks specific detail; nouns that refer to objects or ideas that cannot be observed by the senses, e.g., belief, luck, memory; a summary or statement of the contents of a journal article

ambiguity
uncertainty or lack of clarity in meaning; may result from unclear pronoun references or vague or abstract words or phrases

analysis
careful examination of a cause, effect, process, or product; suggests involvement of precise thought and logic

angle
the perspective or point of view a writer takes and the way in which he or she narrows the topic

annotation
a short evaluative summary of a text added to a bibliography

argument
an idea that has two sides: one for, one against the idea; an argument is the opinion expressed by the writer of an argumentative essay

argumentative essay
an essay written to convince readers to agree with the opinion expressed by the writer

audience
a group of listeners or readers

B

bias
a mental attitude for or against an idea, person, or object

bibliography
a list of sources related to a given topic; the list is arranged according to one of several widely used formats

C

causal chain (*see also* **chain order, cause and effect**)
a series of causes and effects linked closely, one to the other, in chronological or process order

cause and effect
a method of development (in a paragraph or a longer text) that shows what produced an effect or result and the reason for an event or state

chain order
see causal chain

characteristics (e.g., of paraphrases)	typical features
chronological order	a method of development (in a paragraph or a longer text) that shows the order in which things or events occur; chronological order may move from past to present or, if in reverse chronological order, from present to past
citation	a reference to or quotation of a source
classification	a method of development in which ideas or objects are arranged according to the class they belong to
coherent	easy to understand; logically connected
colloquial expressions	words and phrases used in everyday informal language
comparison	a method of development (in a paragraph or a longer text) that looks at similarities between two ideas or objects
conclusion	a last statement that summarises or brings together the main points of a text; sometimes includes a restatement of the topic or thesis sentence
conjunction	a word that connects parts of sentences or phrases, e.g., but, and
connectives	words or phrases that link two ideas or sentences; also called transitions
connotation	an idea suggested by or associated with a word or phrase in addition to its basic or literal meaning, e.g., a person might be referred to as "slim" (positive connotation) rather than "thin" (negative connotation)
consistency	following the same format or form
contractions	shortened or combined words, often words in which an apostrophe takes the place of a vowel, e.g., I'm, can't, wasn't, etc.
contrast	a method of development (in a paragraph or a longer text) that looks at differences between two ideas or objects
convention	widely accepted practice, e.g., the format of a business report

D

definition	a method of development (in a paragraph or a longer text) that defines a term or idea
demonstratives	words that point to or specify the person or thing referred to, e.g., this/these, that/those
denotation	the basic or literal meaning and the counterpart of *connotation*

description, descriptive	a method of development (in a paragraph or a longer text) that describes an idea or object, gives a picture in words
detail or specific detail	supporting information that is concrete and non-general
digression	an aside; departure from the point under discussion
direct quotation	someone's exact words, written or spoken
documentation	supporting evidence from sources
draft (first or rough)	a preliminary version of a text
endnote or footnote	a reference or comment given at the end of a text (or at the bottom of a page for a footnote)
explanation	something that clarifies or interprets an idea; can take the form of a definition, example, specific detail
expository	writing that explains something
fact	a verifiable point used as evidence to explain or support a main idea
figure of speech	an expression with an unusual or idiomatic meaning; includes metaphor, personification, simile
final draft	a complete, carefully revised, and edited version of a written text
first draft	initial or rough copy of a text
focus	a narrowed topic suitable for development into a paragraph or longer text
footnote or endnote	a reference or comment given at the bottom of a page (or at the end of a text for an endnote)
formal writing	a type of writing that employs traditional rules and conventions of grammar; it avoids items like contractions, colloquial expressions
format	the physical layout or arrangement of a text

G

generalisation	a general statement, principle, or opinion that refers to a class, category, order; generalisations should be supported with specific details
genre	a type of text, e.g., business writing, academic writing, novel

I

indent or indentation setting (something) in from the margin; typically text at the beginning of the first line in a paragraph

informal writing writing that uses colloquial language; may include contractions and conversational language; rarely used in academic and professional writing

introduction the first part of a paragraph or longer text; intended to announce the topic and attract readers' attention

irrelevant detail an idea or point that is not important

L

literal following the usual or exact meaning of a word or group of words

M

mechanics the technical details of a written text; includes spelling, punctuation, capitalisation

metaphor a figure of speech that suggests likeness by talking about one thing as if it were another

N

narration a method of development (in a paragraph or longer text) that tells a story narrowing a topic to make a topic more specific and more clearly defined

O

opinion personal belief or point of view (as opposed to a fact)

order the presentation of ideas in a paragraph or longer text, e.g., chronological, spatial, order of importance

order of importance a method of development (in a paragraph or longer text) that presents the most important point first; reverse order of importance would present the least important point first; a frequently used variation is to present the second most important point first, while the remaining points are presented from least to most important

organisation the way in which the different parts of a paragraph or a longer text are put together and connected

outline a skeleton or framework for a longer text

P

paragraph   a group of sentences that focus on one main idea; a paragraph begins on a new line

paragraph patterns/ paragraph development   the structure of a paragraph; the method of development used to present and support a main point

parallel forms   two forms that follow the same pattern, e.g., *Holding* down a job during the day and *studying* at night can lead to sleep deprivation.

paraphrase   to put someone's spoken or written words into one's own words while retaining the original meaning

paraphrasing   expressing someone else's ideas in one's own words

PAT Principle   the sequence of purpose, audience, and topic that should be considered by writers before they develop the first draft of a text

peer   one's equal, a fellow student or colleague

peer feedback   the suggestions a peer, who acts as a reader, offers the writer on his or her text

personification   a figure of speech in which an idea or a thing is represented as a person, e.g., *the idea struck me like an iron fist.*

perspective   the point of view a writer takes and the way in which he or she narrows the topic

phrase   a group of words expressing an idea but lacking a subject and predicate; includes noun, verb, adjective, gerund, infinitive, prepositional phrases

plagiarism   the act of taking ideas or words from a source and presenting them as one's own; careful documentation of the source avoids plagiarism, shows knowledge of relevant literature, and familiarity with conventions

point of view   the way in which something is viewed; the writer's standpoint

predicate   the verb or verb phrase that says something about the subject of a sentence or clause

prewriting   an activity or series of activities, including the brainstorming, discussion, interviewing, reading, and research that is used to prepare for writing

process (*see also* chain of events for cause and effect)   a way of doing something that involves a series of steps

product   the result of the writing process, e.g., a paragraph, an essay

pronouns	a word used to refer to or in place of a noun, including demonstrative (e.g., this, that), interrogative (e.g., who?), personal (e.g., he, you) pronouns
proposition	a statement with which readers may or may not agree (sometimes also called argument, assertion, or premise)
purpose	the intended or desired result, goal

R

reference	a note in a text that refers the reader to the source of information
reference section	list of sources in an academic text
resume	a summary of a job applicant's previous employment experience and education; typically no more than two pages in length
review	to look at something again, possibly with the intention of changing or improving it
revise	to reconsider and rework a text with the intention of improving it
revision	the act of reworking (correcting, improving, bringing up to date) a text to improve it
rhetoric	the art of using words effectively
rhetorical pattern (paragraph pattern)	the structure of a paragraph, the method of development used to present and support a main point
rough draft	initial or first draft of a text

S

scope	the area covered by a topic, activity, or situation
sentence	unit of words in written texts; typically includes a subject and a predicate
sentence structure	the relation of phrases, clauses, and sentence parts within a sentence, e.g., *The bank rate / dropped to its lowest point this year.* (subject) (predicate)
sequence	the order in which ideas or events occur or are arranged
sequential	arranged in continuous order, e.g., alphabetic *a, b, c...* or numeric *1, 2, 3...*
simile	A figure of speech in which one thing or idea is compared to another using *like* or *as*

spatial order	arranged according to space, e.g., from left to right, right to left, top to bottom
subject	the main topic in a paragraph or longer text; a noun, noun phrase, or noun clause in a sentence about which something is said
summary	a shorter form of a text that reflects the main ideas of the original
synonym	a word having the same or almost the same meaning in a given context as that of another word

T

text	a passage of written work
thesis sentence or thesis statement	a statement that states the focus/topic of an argument or opinion put forward and the division of that focus into sub-topics as they wil be developed by reasoned argument; usually used for a longer text
topic	the main focus in a paragraph or longer text
topic sentence or controlling idea	a statement that states the focus/topic of a paragraph; may state the attitude, time, and place of the focus
transitions	words, phrases, or sentences that link one idea with another, either within or between paragraphs; transitions signal to the reader how ideas are related

U

understatement	expressing an idea more weakly than is warranted by its importance, e.g., *Today was not one of the better days of the New York stock market. By the end of trading, the index had dropped to below fifty percent of its opening value.* (Understatement of the gravity of the situation.)
usage	the way in which native speakers typically use a word or phrase; may differ from formal rules of grammar
vague	not clearly or exactly expressed, e.g., *The professor expects students to write many essays* is vague compared to *The professor expects students to write ten essays.*

W

working thesis	a preliminary thesis statement that will be refined as the draft (e.g., of a research paper) is developed

A

Abstractions 39, 40, 58, 199

Academic writing 8, 23, 34, 38, 40, 43, 58, 62, 65, 85, 111, 143

Adjectives 168, 193

Adverbs 193

Agreement 182

Alternating/point-by-point style 47, 49, 54, 89, 95

Ambiguous modifiers 32, 182, 199

Analogies 41, 43

APA style 70, 73, 76, 115, 164

Argumentative essay 11, 117-25, 199

Articles 182

Audience 10-11, 13, 14, 15, 30, 40, 49, 53, 86, 97, 115, 123, 147, 153, 159, 199

B

Bias 199

Bibliographies 106-16, 178, 199
   Annotated 111-16, 199

Block style 20, 47, 49, 54, 89, 95

Brainstorming 9, 38, 42, 50, 72, 76, 85, 86, 94, 103, 113, 115, 147, 150,157

Business reports 141-50

Business writing 34, 58, 149

C

Capitalisation 183

Case 183

Cause and effect 55-56, 180, 199
   causal chain in 57-59, 62, 64, 199
   chronological order in 61, 63
   order of importance in 61, 63

Chicago style 70

Choppy sentences 183

Chronology 180, 200

Citations 72, 80, 200

Classification 35-44, 200

Collective nouns 183

Colloquial expressions 200

Colons 189, 195

Comma fault 183
   splice 184

Commas 183, 184, 194

Comparative forms 184
   adjective 184
   adverb 184

Comparison 11, 41, 45-54, 101, 148, 180, 200

Comparison-and-contrast 45-54, 85, 89-96, 101, 102

Compound object 184

Compound predicate 194

Compound subjects 184

Computers 15, 33, 43, 53, 54, 76, 96, 103-104

Concluding sentences 21, 22, 31, 34, 49, 53, 63, 86, 168

Conclusions 19, 21, 31, 78, 86-89, 93, 95, 96, 124, 168, 180, 200

Conjunctions 200

Connectives 31-34, 120-21, 200

Connectors 31-33, 52, 164

Connotations 200

Contractions 200

Contrast 12, 176, 200

Controlling idea 19, 27, 172, 205

Cover letters 129-40

Cover page 149, 165, 177

D

Dangling modifiers 185

Debatable statements 119, 120, 121

Definitions 35-44, 101, 156, 200

extended 39, 43

short 39, 43

stipulative 40

Demonstratives 33, 200
   pronouns 32

Denotations 200

Dependent clauses 185, 190

Descriptive essay 47

Development 21-28
   by example 22-28
   by point 21-23

Dictionary 42, 76, 96, 164

Digressions 25, 33, 201

Direct objects 185

Documentation 74, 201

Drafts 8, 9, 12-15, 33, 43, 52-54, 61-63, 65, 76, 80, 96, 124, 149, 160-65, 169-71, 201, 204
   First 8, 12-13, 52-53, 63, 160, 162, 163-64, 169, 201
   Rough 12, 63, 96, 201, 204

E

Editing 8, 14-15, 16, 43, 53, 96

Electronic style guides 178

Ellipses 75

Emphasis 21, 74, 181

Essay questions 38, 83-97

Examinations 38, 58

Exclamation points 194

Explaining 11, 21, 39, 57-61, 65, 181

F

Feedback 8, 13-14, 16, 43, 47, 53, 54, 63, 76, 80, 81, 97, 124, 172, 203

Figurative language 41

Figures of speech 201

Final editing 15

Focus 19, 26-29, 37, 63, 103, 157, 168, 201

Footnotes 201

Formal language 11, 146, 149, 153, 188, 201

Formal letters 8

Formatting 8, 14, 43, 65, 139, 143, 168, 201

Fragments 186

Freewriting 10-11

Fused sentences 186

G

Gathering ideas and information 9-10, 26

   techniques for 9-10

Genres 201

GMAT 106, 107

Grammar resources 64, 168

Graphs 57, 62-63, 65, 149

GRE 106, 107

I

Illustrations 51, 63, 101, 181

Indentation 20, 202

Independent clauses 186

Informal writing 188, 202

Informing 11, 94

Internet resources 65, 106, 124, 129

Introductions 19, 21, 78, 86-89, 92, 95, 115, 121, 124, 143, 167, 171, 202

Irregular verbs 186, 196-98

Irrelevant details 25-26, 74, 202

J

Journal indexes 111

Journal writing 9

L

Lab reports 58

Layout 14

Legal documents 40

Length of paragraphs 19

Libraries 65, 76, 106, 124, 129, 131, 160, 175-76

Logical order 31, 33, 61, 63

M

Main clause 186

Main idea 9, 13, 16, 162, 163

Mechanics 8, 14, 32, 70, 124, 168, 169, 202

Metaphors 37, 40-42, 202

Misplaced modifiers 186

MLA style 70

Modal verbs 187

Multi-paragraph essays 20, 21, 85, 143, 150

N

Narration 47, 202

Notecards 160-62, 165

Notetaking 9, 54, 74, 112, 124, 172

O

Order of importance 61, 202

Organising 11, 12, 13, 156, 202

Outline 9, 30, 31, 51, 54, 76, 90, 96, 97, 101, 146-47, 149, 154, 162-63, 165, 202

P

Paragraphs 11, 17-34, 47, 49, 53, 77, 86, 102, 107, 119, 143, 154, 163, 168, 203

   comparison and contrast 47, 49, 102

   organisation of 20-33, 86

   patterns in 21-24, 28, 47, 102, 203

Parallel forms 32, 185, 203

Parallel structure 187

Paraphrasing 69, 74, 76, 77, 80, 81, 161, 165, 200, 203

Parenthetical references 81

Passive voice 187

PAT Principle 10-11, 13, 95, 160, 203

Peers 8, 9, 13-15, 31, 33, 43, 47, 53, 76, 80, 82, 92, 96, 97, 106, 114, 115, 122, 139, 153, 160, 172, 203

Periods 194

Personification 203

Perspective 14, 203

Persuading 119

Phrases 12, 72, 188, 203

Plagiarism 69, 74-76, 203

Point-by-point pattern of comparison 47, 52, 89

Point format 7, 30, 146

Point of view 203

Portfolios 173

Possessives 187

Predicates 203

Prepositions 188

Prewriting 8, 9-12, 13, 15, 29, 49-50, 63, 203

Process writing 8, 15, 203

Pronoun-antecedent agreement 188

Pronouns 32-33, 188, 204

Proofreading 8, 14

Publishing 8, 15, 16, 125

Punctuation 14, 65, 71, 149, 164, 168, 194-95

Q

Question marks 194

Questions 99-108, 161

   analyzing 101

   essay 101-105

   fill-in-the gap 105-106

   multiple-choice 105-106

   sentence-completion 105-106

   short-answer 101-105

   "wh-" 10

Quotations 74-77, 161, 201

   in-line 75

   set-off 74, 75

Quoting 69, 73, 74-75, 80, 86, 165

R

Rearranging details 12, 13

Reference sections 70, 72, 76, 80, 203

Reference sources, *see* Sources

References, list of 70, 111, 156, 158, 161, 165, 204

Reports 8, 40

Research papers 40, 58, 151-65

Resumes 129-40, 204

    chronological 129, 130, 135, 137

    contents of 130

    extracurricular references in 135-36

    format of 130, 137

    functional 129, 137

    purpose of 129, 130

Revisions 8, 13-15, 23, 33, 43, 53-54, 64, 163-64, 169, 204

Rewriting 8, 13, 80

Rhetorical patterns 204

Roman numerals 162

Run-on sentences 97, 189

S

Semicolons 194

Sentence fragments 190

Sentence structure 11, 53, 72, 204

Sequence of ideas 19, 23-25, 29, 33, 204

Similes 37, 40-42

Sources 65, 67-81, 109-15, 153, 160

    see also Bibliography, References

Spatial order 205

Spellchecker 15, 33, 43, 53, 54, 96, 116, 164

Spelling 8, 10, 12, 14, 53, 96, 137, 143, 149, 164, 168

Split infinitive 190

Subject-verb agreement 191

Subjunctive mood 191

Subordinate clauses 191

Summarising 21, 54, 63, 69, 75, 77-81, 101, 115, 116, 205

Superlatives 191

Supporting statements 13, 19, 21, 22, 39, 53, 63, 77, 79, 80, 85, 111, 123, 149, 161, 162, 168

Synonyms 205

T

Tables 62, 65

Tense shifts 192

Thesaurus 42

Thesis statement 9, 11, 21, 76-79, 86, 88, 93, 95, 96, 107, 119-21, 153, 160, 161, 163, 168, 172, 205

Time limits 106-107, 108

Title pages 143, 168

TOEFL 106, 107, 111

Topic sentences 9, 11, 13, 19, 21, 22, 26-28, 30, 34, 37, 47, 49, 51, 53, 54, 59, 63, 78, 79, 80, 86, 94, 102, 107, 119, 124, 153, 205

Transitions 21, 31-33, 47, 49, 52, 53, 76-77, 104, 120-21, 168, 180-81, 204

Transitive verbs 192

Turabian style 70

Typing conventions 71

Typographical errors 137, 143

U

Understatements 205

V

Vagueness 205

Venn diagrams 47, 50

Verbs 72, 81, 129, 167, 168, 189

Vocabulary 11, 72, 74, 164, 168

W

"Wh-" questions 10

Wordiness 115, 192

Word order 192-93

Word processors 15, 53, 164

World Wide Web 8, 27, 65, 70, 111, 125, 178-79

Writing centres 178-79